Technology
Disaster
Response
and Recovery
Planning

Technology Disaster Response and Recovery Planning

A LITA Guide

EDITED BY

Mary Mallery

An imprint of the American Library Association

CHICAGO   2015

MARY MALLERY is the associate dean for technical services at Montclair State University Library. She has published articles and presented on library technology-related topics extensively. She is the book review editor for the *Journal of Electronic Resources Librarianship* and a regular contributor to the Web Review column of *Technical Services Quarterly*. She teaches classes in database design and management as well as metadata sources for library professionals at the Rutgers University School of Communication and Information as a part-time lecturer.

ISBNs
978-0-8389-1315-4 (paper)
978-0-8389-1339-0 (PDF)
978-0-8389-1340-6 (ePub)
978-0-8389-1341-3 (Kindle)

Library of Congress Cataloging-in-Publication Data
Technology disaster response and recovery planning : a LITA guide / edited by
    Mary Mallery.
        pages   cm
    Includes bibliographical references and index.
    ISBN 978-0-8389-1315-4 (print : alk. paper) 1. Library buildings—Safety
    measures—Planning. 2. Libraries—Information technology—Security measures—
    Planning. 3. Electronic information resources--Management—Planning. 4. Library
    materials—Conservation and restoration—Planning. 5. Data protection. 6. Data
    recovery (Computer science)—Planning. 7. Emergency management—Planning.
    8. Library buildings—United States—Safety measures—Case studies. I. Mallery,
    Mary, editor.
    Z679.7T43 2015
    025.8'2—dc23   2014048260

Cover image © foxie/Shutterstock, Inc. Text composition in the Berkeley and Avenir typefaces.

This paper meets the requirements of ANSI/NISO Z39.48–1992 (Permanence of Paper).

⊗ Printed in the United States of America

19 18 17 16 15   5 4 3 2 1

Contents

■ PART 2 ■

Managing Techmageddon:
Disaster Mitigation and Lessons Learned

1

Creating the Technology Disaster Response and Recovery Plan

Chapter One

What Could Go Wrong?
Libraries, Technology, and Murphy's Law

Mary Mallery

L ibraries depend more and more on technology to provide essential services. There are Internet and social media sites, electronic resources, and digital collections; our staff and public infrastructures of PCs, tablets, laptops, and peripherals; and of course the ubiquitous integrated library system (ILS). As technology becomes more essential to everyone's life, this variety of devices, data, and software will grow more complex, as will the many ways that disasters, both natural and manmade, can cause loss of services and resources. Yet most library disaster plans focus on response and recovery from collection and facilities disasters, such as fire and flood.

But how do you begin to draft a comprehensive plan? This LITA Guide will provide readers with a step-by-step, blow-by-blow process to create a Library Technology Disaster Response and Recovery Plan. It includes sample checklists and templates, tools and solutions for promoting collaborative services to enable digital library continuity, and case studies and lessons learned from successful efforts in recovering from library technology disasters.

This LITA Guide includes chapters from contributing authors who have experience and practical advice to share about various aspects of library technology disaster response and recovery planning. The topic will be of great interest to tech-savvy staff—systems librarians, electronic resources librarians, digital collections librarians, data management librarians, emerging technology librarians, and library administrators—as well to librarians who wish to transition into these new careers and to library students. The target audience is academic library staff, with librarians and information professionals in other types of organizations as a secondary audience.

DEFINITION OF TERMS

Librarians were the first to create systematic means of indexing and retrieving information, and as such they have always been in the forefront of the use and development of information science technologies. Technology disaster planning has been and continues to be essential to our field. But which technology do we focus on for our plan, and what constitutes a technology disaster? Let's start out by defining our terms.

What Is Technology?

The word *technology* comes from the Greek *techne,* meaning *skill* or *art,* which includes a vast array of possibilities. For example, long ago, fire was a technology. All libraries use technology to do their work these days, and we depend on it. If we don't have a plan to respond and recover and continue our work in the event of technology failure, when the fire goes out, we will be left in the dark. When we talk about library technology, are we referring to the hardware, software, peripheral devices, or everything mechanical? What about the infrastructure, such as the electrical grid or the telecommunications network—the oxygen that makes the fire possible? Or what about the data—the fuel that makes the fire burn long or fizzle out? These days, when we talk about technology in the library, we talk about *systems,* because technology is not just one device or program but a complex integrated network of many technologies that depend on one another to work effectively.

What Is a Disaster?

The word *disaster* comes from the Latin for "ill-starred." In the old days, a disaster was considered to be the predetermined outcome of inevitable bad luck. These days, however, we believe in self-determination, and that planning will keep away bad luck. Or, as Cassius says to Brutus in Shakespeare's *Julius Caesar,* "The fault, dear Brutus, is not in our stars, but in ourselves." Today, we can plan to moderate the effects of disasters and create networks of experts and services that will help us to respond efficiently and recover effectively, even if the disaster that strikes is not the one we feared.

There are many kinds and causes of disaster, both natural and manmade. There are large-scale natural disasters, such as the 2011 tsunami in Japan that caused the Fukushima disaster, and small failures of technology design, such as the O-ring failure that caused the Challenger explosion in 1986. Large or small, natural or manmade—in complex systems, all the dominoes will fall in a cascade because of one tipping point failure.

Disasters are not just physical phenomena; they affect the whole system. There-fore, a holistic approach and an understanding of the dependencies of modern life are essential to a good disaster plan. Both the environmental and emotional effects of a disaster must be taken into account in planning.

MURPHY'S LAW

When we talk about disasters, we usually think of fire, floods, or earthquakes, but technology disasters can have many more causes than these. The problem can be as simple as ants blocking up a circuit board or "bugs" in the system, but if it causes the system to fail, and we depend on that system, the results can be disastrous.

The story goes that what is known as Murphy's Law was first coined by an American aerospace engineer in 1949. The classic version of Murphy's Law is: "Whatever can go wrong will go wrong." Anyone who works with or depends on technology should keep this adage in mind. It also helps to acknowledge that you cannot anticipate all technology failures. You may never know what may cause the next outage, but you can try to be prepared to mitigate the circumstances so that it does not turn into a disaster.

KINDS OF TECHNOLOGY AND FAILURES

The Y2K bug was the first time that my library's systems department became aware of how much we depended on software and time-stamped databases to maintain our operations, from the integrated library system to the human resources payroll system to even the elevators in the building.

In the twenty-first century, library technology has expanded to include global networks, and as the scope of the technology becomes larger and more complex, the dependencies that our systems rely on for day-to-day operation become more at risk of single and multiple points of failure.

My library has a Collections Disaster Response Plan, which we update on a regular basis. Recently we had an unanticipated technology disaster when there was an air-conditioning outage in the university server room, which caused us to lose access to our digital collections. The consequences of this simple problem had a huge impact on user access to resources, which made us realize how much the library depends on technology to deliver services and host resources. These days, all libraries need a Technology Disaster Response and Recovery Plan in addition to a Collections Disaster Response Plan.

BACKGROUND LITERATURE

The literature on disaster planning for library print collections is well-established and continues to grow. When I searched for model technology disaster response and recovery plans, I found that there was a great deal of literature that focuses on library collections (e.g., Miriam Kahn's classic *Disaster Response and Planning for Libraries*[1] which was updated in 2012 to include more information about library technology systems, electronic resources, digital communications, and social media). However, I found very little library literature technology disaster response and recovery planning.

There are many more technology-focused resources in business literature, such as the American Management Association's *Disaster Recovery Handbook*.[2] Librarians could learn a great deal from business managers, but the library universe's dependence on technology—especially on cloud-based databases—makes the literature of information management systems even more relevant.

National organizations, such as the Heritage Preservation Trust, the Conservation Center for Art and Historic Artifacts (CCAHA), and the Northeast Document Conservation Center (NEDCC), offer workshops and online tools to assist libraries and cultural heritage communities with risk assessment and response and recovery planning for print collection disasters. For example, NEDCC received an Institute of Museum and Library Services (IMLS) grant to create the online tool dPlan, which is profiled in chapter 3. Most recently, the National Network of Libraries of

Medicine has begun the NN/LM Emergency Preparedness and Response Initiative, which provides free online workshops and templates for disaster risk assessment and emergency planning.

FIRST STEPS IN TECHNOLOGY DISASTER RESPONSE AND RECOVERY PLANNING

A one-step-at-a-time approach to disaster response and recovery is optimum. Miriam Kahn introduced the idea that disaster response entails four phases; these are good principles to keep in mind approaching any kind of disaster. They are:

- Phase 1: Respond to Notification
- Phase 2: Assess the Damage
- Phase 3: Begin Rescue and Recovery
- Phase 4: Recovery Process: Resumption of Services; Restoration of Cash Flow; Recovery of Materials[3]

In contrast, in technology and systems administration, Disaster Response and Recovery Plans are split into three parts: Mitigation, Continuity, and Recovery. The UCLA Social Science Data Archive Disaster Recovery Plan presents one of the best examples and offers this explanation of the three main sections:

> The first section, Mitigation, outlines activities the Data Archive will undertake to ensure emergency preparedness and to protect its assets. These activities include risk assessment, an inventory of assets and equipment, backup policies and procedures, standards, training, and the maintenance of the plan.
>
> The second section, Continuity, is concerned with the activities the Data Archive will undertake to ensure continued access to its products and services with minimal disruption in the event of an emergency. This section contains a list of important contacts, references, and relevant department, and campus documents that outline specific emergency procedures.
>
> The final section, Recovery, details the steps the Data Archive will undertake to restore full functionality after an emergency. This section

includes guidance on restoring and using key applications and technologies.[4]

Chapters 2 through 4 in Part 1 of this LITA Guide will help you work through these steps one at a time to build and maintain a Library Technology Disaster Response and Recovery Plan based on this three-part structure. Part 1's concluding chapter provides an in-depth look into future trends in cloud computing in library technology and maps out its role in disaster mitigation, response, and recovery planning.

You don't need a different plan for every technology your library uses, but you do need a comprehensive Technology Disaster Plan that:

1. provides an inventory of technology (hardware, software, and data) with a risk assessment for each
2. describes simple incremental prevention and restoration procedures for each risk
3. identifies training and communication procedures for the plan
4. schedules the iterative process of reviewing and updating the plan on a regular basis

Part 2 of this LITA Guide focuses on practical uses of library technology disaster planning, or what I like to call "Managing Techmageddon." Two experienced professionals provide detailed case studies of recent large-scale technology disasters and discuss how lessons learned have helped to improve technology disaster planning for libraries.

You never know when or how disaster might strike, but with a Technology Disaster Response and Recovery Plan that is integrated into your library's budget and strategic planning policies, your staff will know what procedures and accommodations are in place to weather the storm, and you can be confident that library services will be disrupted as little as possible as a result of any disaster that may come your way.

NOTES

1. Miriam B. Kahn, *Disaster Response and Planning for Libraries,* 3rd ed. (Chicago: ALA Editions, 2012).

2. Michael Wallace and Lawrence Webber, *The Disaster Recovery Handbook: A Step-by-Step Plan to Ensure Business Continuity and Protect Vital Operations, Facilities, and Assets* (New York: American Management Association, 2004).

3. Kahn, *Disaster Response.*

4. UCLA Social Science Data Archive Disaster Recovery Plan (August 2010), p. 4–5, www.sscnet.ucla.edu/issr/da/_images/Disaster.Recovery.Plan.docx.

RESOURCES

IFLA Preservation Section Disaster. Preservation and Conservation. Useful Resources. www.ifla.org/preservation-and-conservation/useful-resources.

Kahn, Miriam B. *Disaster Response and Planning for Libraries,* 3rd ed. Chicago: ALA Editions, 2012.

Library of Congress: Emergency Preparedness, Response, and Recovery website. www.loc.gov/preserv/emergprep.

National Network of Libraries of Medicine (NN/LM) Library Disaster Readiness Test. http://nnlm.gov/ep/2014/08/05/how-ready-is-your-library.

New Jersey State Library Disaster Planning Resources. www.njstatelib.org/services_for_libraries/resources/disaster_planning.

Northeast Document Conservation Center (NEDCC) Emergency Response Framework for the Cultural Community COSTEP). www.nedcc.org/free-resources/costep. The COSTEP Framework is a planning tool designed to bring together cultural institutions with emergency management agencies and first responders. It provides a blueprint for preparing for area-wide disasters and building alliances with federal, state, and local emergency management agencies.

Tanner, Simon. "Do You Understand Your Digital Ecosystem?" *When the Data Hits the Fan* (blog). September 26, 2014. http://simon-tanner.blogspot.co.uk/2014/09/do-you-understand-your-digital-ecosystem.html.

UCLA Social Science Data Archive Disaster Recovery Plan. August 2010. www.sscnet.ucla.edu/issr/da/_images/Disaster.Recovery.Plan.docx.

Wallace, Michael, and Lawrence Webber. *The Disaster Recovery Handbook: A Step-by-Step Plan to Ensure Business Continuity and Protect Vital Operations, Facilities, and Assets.* New York: American Management Association, 2004.

Chapter Two

Inventory and Risk Assessment for Digital Collections

Liz Bishoff and Thomas F. R. Clareson

The threats, vulnerabilities, impacts, and uncertainties that can put libraries and archival collections at risk have multiplied in recent years because the amount of data we interact with has grown exponentially, and the carrier media and playback equipment needed for digital collections has a much shorter life expectancy than those of previous paper collections. However, despite tales of data loss due to corruption of media, and concerns arising from the monumental growth in the amount of digital media, library administration and senior management have not prepared their institutions to address digital preservation and digital collection disaster planning programmatically. Using risk assessment for digital program planning and decision-making can allow libraries and archives to "think globally" about risks, and "act locally" to understand the vulnerabilities of a particular local digital initiative.

To address the issue of risk to digital collections, we must first understand the level of risk. Undertaking a risk assessment can help us to determine the risks across a range of areas, including organizational commitment, financial responsibility, and technical responsibility. Tools and strategies exist to help us identify and manage the risks and expansion of existing institutional and collaborative disaster plans, and programs that support the continuity of operations will ensure the long-term access to digital collections.

RISKS TO DIGITAL COLLECTIONS

Risk assessment is the process of measuring or assessing risk, developing strategies to manage it, and determining the quantitative and/or qualitative value of risk related to a concrete situation and a recognized threat.

There are many types of risk that can harm, or even destroy, digital collections. When discussing risk, what immediately comes to mind are those risks associated with technology, such as hardware and software failures. Next come Acts of God (sometimes referred to as *Force Majeure*), events that are a result of the elements of nature and cannot be reasonably anticipated or controlled, which include damages associated with fires, flooding, and severe weather events.

However, there are other risks to digital collections. Some of these can be anticipated and potentially even controlled, and others are impossible to control.

Organizational changes to libraries and archives can have a major impact on digital programs that put digital collections at risk. Administrative supporters of an institution's digital programs, and the experts who help to build them, can come and go in this age of rapid job and career changes. These disruptions in staffing and organization can impact the resources (both financial and personnel) that support digital initiatives.

Sociocultural views of the importance of cultural heritage can have political consequences that may both directly and indirectly impact support for digital collections. A governor, senator, or representative who is supportive of libraries and archives may drive funding for these initiatives; a governor or legislator who is not can quickly end funding for digital management and preservation programs, leaving repositories scrambling for resources. Many libraries and archives have a legislative mandate to provide long-term access to their digital collections. A thorough understanding of that mandate is critical in building support for digital preservation, identifying and working with your audience or "designated community," and developing the financial structure to protect your digital assets from immediate or long-term loss.

Failure to create a business plan for sustaining a digital preservation initiative can be another major risk to the program. For instance, state legislatures frequently pass legislation that requires a library or archive to implement programs, but do not provide the financial resources needed to do so. Such legislative mandates carry with them inherent legal risks for the organization.

It is necessary to understand the contract and legal ramifications associated with content being digitized or ingested into your digital repositories, and the commitments you make to those who may deposit materials in your digital repositories and archives.

THE IMPACT OF RISK ON DIGITAL COLLECTIONS

When a digital collection is at risk, librarians and archivists may focus first on potential damage to, or loss of, digital assets, but there are many other impacts that go beyond the actual collections. Depending on the seriousness of the failure of the digital system, the reputation of the staff managing the repository could be damaged.

The lack of availability of digital content due to a disaster or a security incident may result in a statutory breach of duty, where an organization is failing to carry out legally mandated responsibilities. In many states and countries, mandates for regulatory compliance that govern the protection of confidential information from data breaches already exist.

Although the loss of digital data may not cause direct financial liability, there may be significant financial impacts on the funds spent in attempts to recover the data. Another concern is whether the library or archive has an obligation to authenticate, render, and verify a digital resource a digital resource—the primary purpose of digital preservation.

Risk assessment will help your organization to determine the likelihood of any possible threats or impacts. Does your organization have a high, medium, or low vulnerability to a certain risk? For instance, if your institution does not have a legislative or statutory mandate to retain a particular digital collection, then you will have a lower risk associated with the loss of data. If the collection that is created doesn't utilize any commercial software for content creation, then the risk of contractual liability will be low.

An important early step in risk assessment is to clarify any organizational mandates to provide long-term access to the collection. Are you legally required to make the digital information accessible? Is there an institutional mandate to provide specific information included in your bylaws or articles of incorporation? Or is there a professional or ethical mandate that requires you to provide the information to a specific audience? Rather than considering these mandates to be threats, consider them helpful "building blocks" for constructing digital disaster plans and overall digital preservation policies. The public service and information technology (IT) departments should document the following issues for review by senior management and boards:

13

- What type of mandate supports the long-term access and preservation of your digital collections?
- How can, or how does, your organization demonstrate commitment to those mandates?
- How can you further build commitment?

BUILDING THE COMMITMENT TO DIGITAL PRESERVATION

You can measure your organization's commitment by documenting any mandates in formal, written commitment statements or policies. Your policies on digital preservation and disaster planning should be based on answers to the following questions:

- Who will use digital collections and repository services? In other words, who are the target users of your digital content? In the Open Archival Information System (OAIS) Reference Model that forms the cornerstone of many institutional digital preservation policies, these users are called a "designated community." OAIS defines this as "an identified group of potential Consumers which should be able to understand a particular set of Information [that] may be composed of multiple user communities"—the set of users for which the digital content is being preserved so that they can use it in the future.[1]
- What digital content will be collected?
- How long will it be kept?
- How long is access required? Is the period for which the material must be retained short-term (one to three years), medium-term (three to seven years), or long-term (permanent)?
- What type of access services will be offered?

If this type of information is documented in writing, that is another risk to the continued availability of your digital assets.

INVENTORYING DIGITAL COLLECTIONS

Identifying all formats in your digital collection is an important early step in the development of a digital preservation plan and should be incorporated into your digital disaster plan. Your institution should create a comprehensive list of file formats in the digital library's care. Lack of easy access to such a list makes it difficult to plan your digital preservation program.

One way to start bringing this information together is for library or archive staff to ask the IT staff to pull a list of digital holdings by the format and/or type of material your organization creates and acquires.

Because individuals in your organization may be managing collections on their own systems (i.e., on individual computers that aren't on the main network), it is helpful to conduct a survey to identify these and gather information on the file formats, hardware, and software required to support them. This inventory process will allow you to analyze the contents of your collections and record the number of individual files. In addition to a list by file format (e.g., JPEG, TIFF, WAV), you may want to document the type of digital objects being created. These can include photographs and other still images; simple text; encoded text (e.g., blogs, websites, and listservs); non-licensed e-books and e-journals; digital audio; digital video; art or visual materials with a database component; applications, operating systems, or other software; documentation or research data; and geospatial data. Other components of your digital assets and environment to inventory include the number of files; the software, hardware, and operating system used to create the assets; the institution's overall hardware, software, and operating environment; the age and maintenance records of equipment used in digital library operations; and the metadata available to support your digital resources. Some libraries and archives may take a proactive position in their campuses or municipalities by inventorying the digital collections held across the overall community setting.

At the same time you are conducting the inventory, you may want to analyze your digital collection based on the characteristics of the resources they include. Identify materials that are at a high risk of loss, including:

- low-redundancy assets, for which few or no copies exist
- digital assets for which there is no concern for the ongoing access to or preservation of the physical collections

15

- digital materials created on proprietary systems, that is, systems where the source code is closed or available on a limited basis (e.g., a proprietary system like Microsoft Windows)
- digital materials created in non-standard file formats
- materials where the possibilities of conversion back to an analog format are unlikely, or it would not be preservationally sound to do so; this might include digital objects that rely on hardware and software to be usable (e.g., audio and video materials), or where the vast quantity of data makes analog conversion impossible (e.g., datasets or GIS materials)

ORGANIZATIONAL COMMITMENT

Organizational commitment to digital preservation is an important aspect of digital preservation and disaster planning that is key to sustainability and succession planning. The organization must ask these questions about its digital operations:

- Has the institution implemented an organizational structure that will support its continued commitment to its digital assets?
- Is there a budget that supports this continued commitment?
- Is there a defined exit strategy or succession plan that details what the organization will do if it is no longer able to provide user access to digital resources or support a digital preservation solution for the long term (i.e., return the digital assets to the creators, work with another digital solution organization, etc.)?

Failure to engage in this type of planning may give the impression that your organization will provide a *perpetual* digital preservation service for all its digital resources.

Your institution should also measure its organizational fitness to implement a digital preservation program that includes digital disaster recovery. Create an inventory of current staff skills that details the skills required to implement, operate, and manage the digital preservation program. Although the inventory should be specific to the digital preservation program, most staff are likely to work in a variety of areas beyond digital preservation roles. It may be easiest to have staff inventory *all* of their skills and then emphasize their digital preservation work. The skills that are required for digital preservation and digital disaster recovery will depend on what phase of your digital program you are in. Libraries and archives in the planning stages of digital preservation and digital disaster recovery strategy require staff with different skills (e.g., investigation, research, and communication) than will be needed in the implementation stage (e.g., system operations and data-wrangling skills).

Personnel in libraries and archives with digital collections must remain current on emerging technologies, new formats of digital materials, and fresh concepts. It is important to specify how staff will identify and master skills that will be needed in the future. Plan to provide ongoing training—your organizational commitment to this can be demonstrated through a training plan and budget. The lack of a specific budget or plan for digital preservation training may result in staff who cannot cope with emerging technology.

It requires money to hire and train staff. Your organization should develop a multi-year budget for the digital preservation program that uses generally accepted accounting practices to identify expenses and funding sources. If your organization doesn't have separate budgets for digital initiatives, IT, and preservation, how can it guarantee that the digital collection and/or digital preservation repository will be funded in the future?

The results of a 2011 survey of the research library community by Bishoff[2] revealed some startling findings about digital preservation funding sources. Unit operating budgets and grants were the top sources for funding digital initiatives, which is worrisome because grants rarely provide a *continuing* source of support for these programs. Of greater concern was that 23.6 percent of the survey respondents stated that they do not specifically allocate any funding for IT activities. One organization noted that although it "would like to fund preservation of our digital collections via the IT budget of our parent agency . . . at this point in time, there is no system in place to address digital preservation within the larger agency."[3]

Finally, consider that your organization will need to maintain legal and contractual rights to its digital collections. You need to create an inventory of contracts, legal agreements, and legislative mandates, and determine if you have the resources to support the regulatory framework or legislative requirements. What are the societal, ethical, judicial, or other governance requirements your organization must meet? Examples of the types of contracts and legal agreements include, on the federal level, copyright and indigenous peoples legislation, and contractual agreements that include maintenance of donor agreements, deeds of gift, and software licenses. Are there standards or voluntary codes that your institution needs to comply with? These could include "industry standards" or best practices that ensure long-term access to collections, and voluntary codes such as Repository Operating Manuals or Preferred Ingest File Format listings. Failing to comply with these requirements can put your organization's digital collections at risk.

While you are doing the staff skills inventory, also consider how the loss of key staff would impact planning or development of your digital preservation repository or disaster planning strategy. If you are funding these key positions through "soft money" such as grants, and have no plans to move staff to your organization's operating budget, this is another risk to the sustainability of your digital collections.

As you look at all these areas of potential risk, it is important for your organization to have a clear policy framework. Does your institution have a tradition of developing policies, reviewing them at regular intervals, and enforcing them? Relying on word of mouth or "policy by oral tradition" will be insufficient in the fast-moving, ever-changing world of digital preservation. Enforcing policies that are not in writing is difficult. Libraries and archives are viewed as inherently trustworthy organizations. Transparency is valued in digital preservation, and it comes about by having written policies that are openly available to management, staff, users, donors, and funders. In the digital environment, the availability of written policies reinforces an institution's trustworthiness to its stakeholder groups.

TECHNICAL INFRASTRUCTURE RISK ASSESSMENT

For those organizations that have implemented a digital preservation program, a risk assessment associated with the technical infrastructure should be undertaken. Common elements of the technical-assessment process include reviews of the technical environment (physical facilities), confirming the quality and currency of the software (i.e., ensuring that the most recent operating system and all updates have been installed), keeping accurate logs, and interviewing staff. The technical assessment will vary if the organization outsources its preservation services: contracts will need to be reviewed, reports should be evaluated, and problem logs should be audited. Organizations that are participating in distributed networked preservation services, such as Private LOCKSS Networks or LOCKSS, will require additional assessment elements to reflect the distributed nature of the service. For those organizations that use open source software, or have developed their own digital preservation service, risk assessment elements related to writing new code or updating existing code may need to be incorporated. Planning for continued product development and funding and staffing the service are key aspects in these environments.

RISK ASSESSMENT SUMMARY

In summary, your risk assessment process should include:

- reviewing your commitment to digital preservation
- identifying and clarifying your institutional mandates
- inventorying your digital assets and environment
- verifying your organizational fitness
- determining your financial infrastructure
- collecting documentation required for planning and decision-making
- ensuring fitness of the technical infrastructure to support the program

TOOLS TO HELP

In the past decade, the library, archival, and data-management communities have developed tools that can help organizations determine the level of risk to which their digital collections are exposed. Several of these tools are specifically designed for risk assessment, whereas others are designed for the broader purposes of audit and certification. In February 2007, OCLC/Research Libraries Group (RLG) and the Center for Research Libraries released *Trustworthy Repositories Audit and Certification: Criteria and Checklist*. This tool was used for planning as well as for audit and certification, until it was superseded by *Audit and Certification of Trustworthy Repositories* (commonly known as the Magenta Book), which is largely used for audit and certification rather than planning or risk assessment.[4]

Several other tools have been specifically designed for risk assessment and can be used in conjunction with the Magenta Book. The Digital Respository Audit Method Based on Risk Assessment (DRAMBORA), developed by the Digital

Curation Centre and DigitalPreservationEurope (www.repositoryaudit.eu), is based on risk assessment and provides a method for self-assessment of digital assets.

More recently, the Digital Curation Centre built on the work of DRAMBORA and developed The Collaborative Assessment of Research Data Infrastructure and Objectives (CARDIO) a "benchmarking tool for data-management strategy development,"[5] which looks at institutional requirements, activity, and capacity in digital curation and digital preservation. This tool was built in response to the growth of data-management needs in universities across the European Union. Using many of the same elements for assessment as DRAMBORA, this tool is designed to be used by teams, allowing for collaborative decision-making as part of the assessment process.

In 2009, the Joint Information Systems Committee (JISC) developed the Assessing Institutional Digital Assets (AIDA) Self-Assessment Toolkit (http://aida.jiscinvolve.org/wp/toolkit) to enable higher education institutions in the United Kingdom to perform self-assessments of capacity, state of readiness, and overall capability for digital asset management. AIDA takes into account the level of institutional preparedness, highlights threats to assets, and recommends remedial options. Although targeted at institutions of higher education in the United Kingdom, AIDA can be used as a guide for others undertaking digital preservation assessment.

NOTES

1. *Audit and Certification of Trustworthy Repositories* (Washington, DC: Consultative Committee for Space Data Systems), June 2012, 111, http://public.ccsds.org/publications/archive/650x0m2.pdf. Another definition of "designated community," and an illustration of how a repository interacts with its designated community, are available in the Portico Designated Communities Feedback Policy, www.portico.org/digital-preservation/wp-content/uploads/2011/03/Portico-Designated-Communities-Feedback-Policy.pdf.

2. Liz Bishoff, Assessing Your Preservation Readiness: An ASCLA Webinar, April 16, 2012.

3. Building Commitment for Long-Term Access to Digital Materials, ACRL Digital Curation Interest Group Webinar, May 22, 2012.

4. *OCLC Trustworthy Repositories Audit and Certification: Criteria and Checklist,* www.crl.edu/sites/default/files/attachments/pages/trac_0.pdf; *Audit and Certification of Trustworthy Repositories.*

5. The Collaborative Assessment of Research Data Infrastructure and Objectives, http://cardio.dcc.ac.uk.

RESOURCES

Consultative Committee for Space Data Systems. *Audit and Certification of Trustworthy Repositories: Magenta Book.* September 2011. http://wiki.lib .sun.ac.za/images/2/22/652x0m1.pdf.

Digital Curation Centre. The Collaborative Assessment of Research Data Infrastructure and Objectives (CARDIO). http://cardio.dcc.ac.uk.

Digital Curation Centre and DigitalPreservationEurope, Digital Repository Audit Method Based on Risk Assessment (DRAMBORA). 2008. www .repositoryaudit.eu/about.

Joint Information Systems Committee (JISC). 2009. http://aida.jiscinvolve.org/ wp/toolkit.

Online Computer Library Center, Inc. (OCLC)/Research Libraries Group (RLG)/ Center for Research Libraries (CRL), *Trustworthy Repositories Audit and Certification: Criteria and Checklist.* 2007. www.crl.edu/sites/default/files/ attachments/pages/trac_0.pdf.

Portico, Designated Communities Feedback Policy. 2011. www.portico.org/ digital-preservation/wp-content/uploads/2011/03/Portico-Designated -Communities-Feedback-Policy.pdf.

Chapter Three

Disaster Planning and Risk Management with dPlan

Donia Conn

The process of disaster planning for digital collections entails a great deal of work, and it can often feel overwhelming. dPlan: The Online Disaster-Planning Tool (www.dplan.org) is an online tool designed for cultural and civic institutions that must create disaster plans. It is not only a template for a collection-wide disaster plan, but also a good training tool which ensures that institutions consider all the factors necessary for a successful response.

The disasters that impact both digital and physical collections can come in any size. As stewards of these collections, we need to be prepared to respond to ensure minimal disruptions to access. A digital disaster can range from simple bit rot on a single file up to full-scale failure of a server. Is it considered it an isolated incident? Will it fix itself over time if just left alone? Can the file be restored with a viable, accessible backup? Whether or not you have already experienced a digital disaster (even a small one), a disaster plan will help you prepare for an incident that destroys data or renders it inaccessible, and documents how you can mitigate and recover from that loss. Documenting, printing, and distributing crucial system and response information via the plan to all relevant staff helps to ensure a thoughtful, timely, and efficient response—regardless of the scope of a disaster.

Planning for any disaster requires devoting a great deal of time to performing assessments and gathering information, but it is time well spent. The first step is to ensure that all the digital collections you have are clearly identified, organized, and described. The next necessary step is to conduct a risk assessment, which encourages institutions to consider possible hazards such as natural disasters, hardware or software failure, security gaps, vendor closure, and obsolescence. Developing a sense of how frequently these events could occur and what impact they might have on digital collections will help to create a more useful plan. (A more complete discussion of risk assessment can be found in chapter 2.)

Disaster planning builds upon the risk assessment. A disaster plan will bring together the people, equipment, and space necessary to respond to an incident. The planning process also includes pre-disaster communications with all involved parties, both within and outside the institution. Building solid relationships before an incident creates an environment that will discourage relying on last-minute decisions; in the event of a disaster, all involved will know exactly what their role will be in meeting institutional priorities. Writing the plan and building these relationships is a major project, but will pay for itself in the event of a disaster. If your institution already has a plan for its physical collections, much of the groundwork will already be laid. Review it carefully to ensure that it includes all necessary information concerning digital collections.

A plan will be invaluable when it is necessary to respond to and recover from a disaster. This chapter will discuss how dPlan can aid in the planning and recovery process. (Planning is covered in greater detail in chapter 4.)

HOW CAN dPLAN HELP?

About dPlan

dPlan was developed in 2005 by the Northeast Document Conservation Center (NEDCC) and the Massachusetts Board of Library Commissioners (MBLC) to provide easy-to-complete templates for collection disaster planning. It is freely available to any institution that wishes to use it. With the assistance of the Institute of Museum and Library Services and the National Center for Preservation Technology and Training, NEDCC and MBLC worked with professionals across the country to create a template suitable for both physical and digital collections. The ease of completing the online forms, the guidance provided throughout, and the plethora of information available in the printed documentation make it a very valuable tool. The template is designed to be filled out online and then printed. This creates a hard copy of the information generated from the responses to the online forms, which is accessible even if there is no power or network capability. Disaster plans

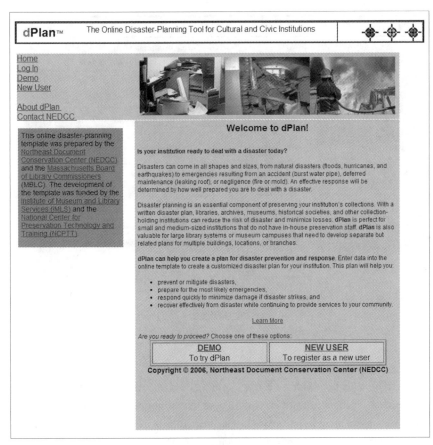

FIGURE 3.1
dPlan home page

created with dPlan are stored on multiple secure servers sponsored by NEDCC to provide additional backup.

dPlan covers all aspects of disaster planning for any type of collection, regardless of whether it is digital or physical. It addresses prevention, response and recovery, supplies and services, and training.

Prevention

In the prevention section, users are encouraged to perform their own risk assessments; record the institution's preventive maintenance procedures; and enter detailed information on the facilities, which includes details about shutoff

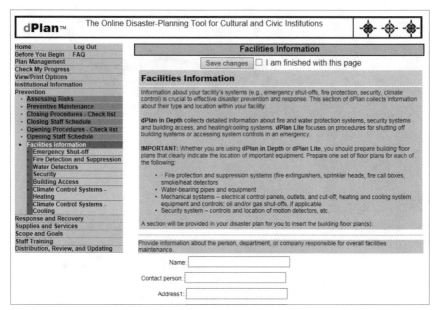

FIGURE 3.2
Sample dPlan page showing list of sections to left

instructions; and fire, water, heating, cooling, and security systems; and contact information for the relevant personnel. Note that although your institution's existing risk assessment and accompanying facilities information may address the institution as a whole—and therefore not include information relevant to your unit—it is nonetheless critical to any disaster plan for digital collections.

Response and Recovery

This section focuses on people and collections. It lists and describes the responsibilities recommended for the disaster response team and encourages the institution to identify people ahead of time to fill these roles. As dPlan advises,

> The members of the disaster team should be able to think clearly under pressure, consider all options quickly but carefully, make decisions, and act. In particular, the head of the team will need to provide strong leadership in stressful circumstances. The composition of the disaster

team may reflect the organizational hierarchy, but in some cases it may be better if it does not.[1]

Although this advice may not always be easy to follow, it is critical to a successful response. This section of dPlan also addresses salvage priorities and insurance information, as well as specifics related to information technology (which will be discussed in greater detail later in this chapter). Salvage priorities, both physical and digital, should be listed by collection and location. Documentation of these priorities can save time and money, and also ensure that the data is accessible as soon as possible. Although not everyone will need to know the details of insurance policies, information about institutional coverage—especially in relation to the hazards identified in the risk assessment—will prevent confusion in the moment.

Supplies and Services

Communication is the real key to disaster planning and response. This section compiles the information needed to facilitate the process. Emergency service information should be listed along with information on utilities (e.g., power and water) and recovery services for physical collections. The dPlan template can accommodate the addition of collection-specific services like data-recovery vendors. Emergency supplies and availability of emergency funds are also covered in this section.

Remaining Sections

The final sections of dPlan include areas in which to describe the scope and goals the institution has for writing the plan, guidance for staff training, and how the institution wants to distribute, review, and update the plan.

USING dPLAN FOR DIGITAL DISASTER PLANNING—EXAMPLES

Because dPlan simplifies the process of drafting a digital disaster plan, it is especially useful for small institutions with limited IT staff. dPlan prompts users to fill in responses to questions rather than having to determine on their own what information is necessary.

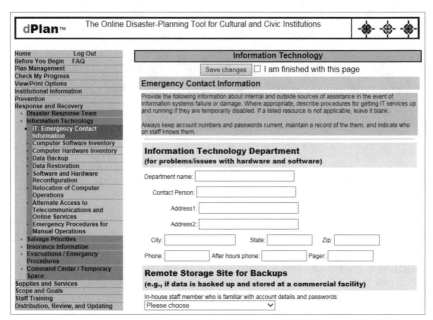

FIGURE 3.3

Sample dPlan page from the Information Technology section of dPlan

Collecting Emergency Contact Information

For those that need guidance, the information technology section begins with a helpful introduction that reviews very basic strategies for protecting digital collections and equipment, including backing up data, setting salvage priorities, and contingency planning for remote access to collections. This section directs the institution to collect emergency contact information for a wide range of people. dPlan prompts users to fill in emergency contact data for IT staff contacts, remote storage site(s) for backups, Internet service providers, web site hosts, online subscription service(s), and regional online catalog/networks.

Creating Hardware and Software Inventories

dPlan also prompts institutions to complete hardware and software inventories. Although this information may already be recorded in other inventories and reports, including it here simplifies access in the event of a disaster by eliminating the need to track down multiple documents. dPlan recommends printing multiple copies and storing them in different locations so information can be retrieved easily even when power and Internet access are unavailable.

An example of the guidance that dPlan provides can be seen in the inventory and data backup sections excerpted below.

Computer Hardware Inventory

In most cases, salvage of collections will be a higher priority than salvage of damaged software and/or computer equipment. Backups and/or insurance coverage will generally provide for replacement of damaged software and hardware. However, an up-to-date inventory of these types of items will be required for insurance purposes.[2]

Data Backup

Identify all electronic data unique to your institution that are maintained solely in-house (e.g., collection records, in-house databases, financial information digital collections). For each, indicate the location of the data, the person responsible for backup, the location of onsite and off-site backup(s) for the data, and the frequency of backup. If any of this data is not currently backed up, devise backup procedures immediately.[3]

The final parts of this IT section compile information about how the institution plans to ensure the continuity of operations, including procedures for restoring data and reconfiguring hardware, relocating computer operations, providing alternative access to telecommunications and online services, and reverting to manual operations. Again, guidance is given in dPlan as demonstrated from data restoration and reconfiguration.

Alternative sites for computer and telecommunications operations are known as "facility backups" in the parlance of contingency planning for commercial businesses. There are several different types of facilities that might be maintained:

- A reciprocal arrangement, where arrangements are made beforehand with a nearby organization that would be willing and able to provide space and equipment to set up computer systems for the institution that has suffered the disaster.

29

- A "cold site," which is a commercially owned building or space with power and air-conditioning, where computers and other equipment would be set up if a disaster occurred. This usually can be set up in a matter of days.
- A "hot site," which is a commercially operated computer facility that is staffed at all times and would have the institution back up and running within hours of a disaster. This option is very expensive and usually not practical for libraries or archives.

If the institution decides to have temporary facilities available for the resumption of computer operations, this must be planned well in advance. The arrangements will not be useful if the necessary equipment and software is not available, not compatible with backup data, or simply doesn't work.[4]

Guidance on providing alternatives for data and telecommunications is also included:

> In the event of an emergency that requires your institution to relocate to an alternate site for a significant period of time, it may be necessary for staff and/or patrons to access email, Internet, and online services (such as the library's website, online catalog, or online subscription databases) from that site. Redirecting existing accounts may do this, or it may be necessary to provide alternative ways to access online resources. In this section, provide appropriate information and instructions for handling such a situation.
>
> Be sure to indicate who within the library has authority to change/move Internet accounts or the library's website. Contact information and account numbers for any outside service providers (e.g., Internet service provider, web hosting service) have been provided in the IT: Emergency Contact Information form.[5]

ADVANTAGES AND DISADVANTAGES OF USING dPLAN

As with any program, dPlan has strengths and weaknesses. It simplifies the process of drafting a digital disaster plan, which is especially useful for small institutions with limited IT staff. It is an excellent program for organizations that have never created a disaster plan because it is designed to guide its users through the steps necessary to create a disaster plan. It offers value-added services such as backup, technical assistance, and advice. And although the structure of the online tool makes it easy to use, it is important to note that dPlan is effective *only* if a hard copy of the completed plan is printed out. The printed version of the plan provides a wealth of information that is not visible in the online form, hence the importance of printing a hard copy.

Its major drawback is its outdated and clunky software (there are plans to update it when funding becomes available). It does not provide sufficient detail to create plans for larger collections and repository systems. Finally, because the plan is designed to be all-encompassing, it is difficult to pull out only the information to create a stand-alone plan.

Nonetheless, dPlan is a useful tool for overall assistance in writing a disaster plan. Its exhaustive online template, supporting documentation, and automatic backup to multiple servers across the United States make it an excellent resource for small institutions just beginning the journey of writing a plan.

NOTES

1. dPlan—The Online Disaster-Planning Tool: Data Collection Forms (2006), 42, www.dplan.org/data_cx_forms_20060831.pdf.

2. Ibid., 49.

3. Ibid., 51.

4. Ibid., 54.

5. Ibid., 55.

RESOURCES

dPlan—The Online Disaster-Planning Tool for Cultural and Civic Institutions. www.dplan.org.

dPlan—The Online Disaster-Planning Tool: Data Collection Forms. 2006. www.dplan.org/data_cx_forms_20060831.pdf.

Massachusetts Board of Library Commissioners. http://mblc.state.ma.us.

Northeast Document Conservation Center. https://www.nedcc.org.

Chapter Four

Disaster Communication
Planning and Executing a Response

Denise O'Shea

A ctive communication is the key to a successful recovery for libraries faced with responding to a disaster. Unfortunately, although communication is one of the human elements of a disaster plan that is often downplayed or overlooked, it remains a critical component of all stages of disaster recovery. To call more attention to the issue, this chapter focuses on the communication element of a technology disaster response.

PRELIMINARY PLANNING

In the planning phase, the disaster team should be selected and the designated spokesperson for internal and external communication should be identified. Although it is not always possible, or even desirable, for a single person to speak for a library during a disaster, it is important that the disaster response team work together to ensure that everyone delivers a consistent message. One of the key responsibilities of the designated spokesperson is to let people know what happened, what is being done to resume service, and what help (if any) is needed. In small libraries, the designated spokesperson for both internal and external communication is typically the library director. In an academic library, it is usually the Library Dean. In larger institutions, the designated spokesperson may be someone outside of the library, such as the public information officer (PIO), or someone with the title of public relations officer or communication officer. If this is the case, the designated spokesperson should handle all external communication and possibly the internal communication as well.

PREPARATION

"One of the important tasks in disaster response and recovery is to coordinate various communication and collaborative efforts with other units and individuals."[1]

After the disaster response team members are selected and the designated spokesperson is identified, a disaster response communication plan should be prepared. The plan must address both internal and external communication. This includes:

- communicating with library staff, the parent institution, the local disaster response network, insurance companies, vendors, contractors, and consultants
- coordinating with computer technical support regarding data backup and recovery
- reporting to stakeholders, funding agencies, and the media.[2] (The list of stakeholders includes your library's patrons, community members, and the library board.)

In order for communication among the disaster response team, library staff, and institution/community emergency responders to be effective, you need to establish and maintain a working relationship before a disaster occurs. Schedule meetings with all parties to outline needs and requirements in order to minimize the confusion, misunderstanding, and miscommunication that can occur during a disaster.

KEY COMPONENTS OF THE COMMUNICATION PLAN

A comprehensive disaster communication plan should contain the following:

a disaster team phone tree that consists of names, responsibilities, phone numbers, alternate phone numbers (home and mobile) and alternate contact information (e.g., personal email addresses), and the order in which the library disaster team should receive calls regarding the disaster

an emergency contact list for library staff

an emergency communication directory that includes contact information for the local disaster response network, utilities, insurance companies, vendors, contractors and consultants, computer technical support, and other essential individuals and agencies

a one-page service continuity plan (see, e.g., the OPAL templates available at http://nnlm.gov/ep/disaster-plan-templates)

basic communication scripts and press releases, including:

- a script that tells staff where to report and who is essential
- a list of media outlets that should receive press releases:

  local TV, radio, and newspapers
  local blogs and websites
  local libraries and archives
  regional library consortium and the state library

a plan to provide updated contact information and library hours to:

- the library and institution websites
- vendors, insurance companies, suppliers, the post office, creditors, etc.
- a library website and social media plan that details how to keep the library website, online resources, and social media accessible and updated.

Phone numbers and other contact information should be tested for accuracy and completeness before a disaster occurs and re-tested at least once per year or whenever a new contact is added to the list. Incomplete or incorrect information can cost valuable time during a disaster. Design basic communication scripts with an eye toward flexibility and be ready to improvise the scripts as needed as it is impossible to predict in advance the form that a disaster will take.

SITUATION AWARENESS REPORTING

Disaster team members should practice reporting *what, when,* and *where* before, during, and after a service disruption as shown in the following examples.

March 8, 2013

- Please remember to dial 924-SNOW tomorrow morning before heading out to work. If the University is closed, all non-essential staff should not report to work. Essential staff will communicate with the Library Director, who will be communicating with the Associate Dean for Public Services.

- Due to the many uncertainties of this storm, it's hard to tell at this time what conditions will be like during the morning commute. Most of the forecasts I've seen show snow throughout the day, so even if we can open the library, we may be in an early, closing scenario. However, we'll have to let it play out and make adjustments along the way.

- The Service Continuity Team (SCT) and essential services staff are now on stand-by. Essential services staff from the standpoint of staffing the library and the SCT from the standpoint of keeping our core services available from their homes. Because there is the potential for power outages, the Head of Reference will coordinate the SCT. If you are on the SCT and you lose power during business hours, please contact the Head of Reference. She will then notify a backup, if one is available.

- The Library's Webmaster will be handling messages on the library's website, and will be in communication with our social media maven, the Head of Access Services. Therefore it is essential that the Webmaster is made aware of any changes to our hours.

Adapted from Ports in a Storm, njstatelib.org/services_for_libraries/resources/disaster_planning/ports_in_storm.

COMMUNICATION CHALLENGES AND SOLUTIONS

"Disasters can disrupt both the physical communication networks and the social networks that are critical to efficient response and recovery."[3]

A disaster creates a demand for information. Library stakeholders may not know what happened, but they want information. They also want to be informed about the progress of the recovery. Maintaining open lines of communication during a disaster is one of the critical components of the disaster communication plan. A quick response fills the information vacuum that occurs during the disaster and helps to create the perception that the library is in control of the situation. However, the communication infrastructure—both the technical infrastructure and the social infrastructure—is frequently one of the hardest hit areas during a disaster, and this can slow down or impede an effective communication response.

FAILED PHYSICAL COMMUNICATION CHANNELS

All physical communication networks are vulnerable to power outages. In a large-scale natural disaster, the traditional means of communication—telephone lines, cell phone networks, and Internet service providers (ISPs) may be negatively impacted by a heavy demand on limited resources. This means that institutional email and websites, including the library website, may be unavailable. All of this makes the ability to provide a quick and effective response difficult. It may also mean limited or no access to library tools and resources such as the library catalog, EZProxy, electronic databases, and other electronic resources (e.g., e-books, or streaming audio and video). Your communication plan should consider how your library will communicate and provide access to your library's electronic resources during a large-scale or long-term disaster when the communication infrastructure may be compromised. Kahn[4] recommends that you get advice from your institution's emergency management or public safety office concerning methods of communication during a disaster.

Critical components of your library's disaster communication plan should include backup plans for failed communication channels, including alternate channels of communication (substituting online chat or text messaging for in-person reference services) or redundant communication channels (e.g., storing disaster plan documents on a remote server that is protected from the effects of local calamities such as floods and power failures). The Internet, remote hosting services, and cloud-based technology solutions have made it easier for libraries to build backup and redundancy into their disaster communication plans. Using cloud-based applications for disaster response means that members of disaster response teams can access their information from wherever they may be located with fewer delays and interruptions.

FAILED SOCIAL COMMUNICATION CHANNELS

In the event of a large-scale disaster, displacement of library staff and disaster responders can become a huge issue. Finding and keeping track of where staff members are located is extremely important, but it can be very time-consuming and can slow down your disaster response. Where are they? Do they need help with heat, housing, electricity, transportation, child care, etc.? Where and when should they report to work, or should they just stay home? Staff members and disaster team members may be affected by physical or emotional wellness issues, including stress and low morale. Furthermore, during a disaster the disaster response team may be geographically dispersed, which may make it difficult for the team to collaborate efficiently and effectively.

LESSONS LEARNED FROM THE FIELD OF CRISIS COMMUNICATION

Despite all of the potential problems outlined in this section, you must remember that disaster does not equal silence! Silence leads to an information vacuum. No communication with your staff will result in people gathering information from unofficial sources, and they will base their behavior on untrustworthy data. Unclear communication may result in panic or hesitation.

In the face of these challenges, disaster team members must strive to be:

- quick to respond
- able to project confidence
- prepared
- patient, flexible, and ready to forgive errors
- consistent and frequent in their communications—keep people informed and help keep them calm, and deliver messages that are free of contradictions
- open and willing to talk to stakeholders and the media about the disaster
- ready to make specific requests that clearly describe what others can do to help
- able to put the team front and center and demonstrate a unified front

SOCIAL MEDIA—AN OPPORTUNITY AND A CHALLENGE

Social media and web-based applications offer a variety of options for sharing information and collaborating on projects such as disaster response. Social networking tools and mobile devices are great options for providing reference services when power and/or phone lines are down. Although social media presents a number of options for use in sharing information, there can be issues with maintaining control over content in order to keep the focus and quality of information consistent. A solid disaster communication plan that incorporates the effective use of social media can help a library make the most of these tools during a crisis.

Free Web-Based and Social Media Applications for Disaster Response

Social media and web-based applications can be useful for disaster response by expediting internal and external disaster response and recovery collaboration; providing redundancy and backup communication channels; enabling the remote updating of critical disaster documents (e.g., the disaster manual or plan); allowing staff to contribute to disaster response and recovery planning, regardless of where they are located; and maintaining a two-way dialogue with library patrons and other stakeholders

These applications include:

- instant messaging, chat, Twitter, and Facebook for reference services
- Twitter to seek volunteers for help with disaster recovery
- Skype or Google Hangout for collaboration and real-time meetings
- Google Drive, Dropbox, and Evernote for document sharing information
- MailChimp and Gmail for free email services and newsletters

Most of these applications are free or available at low cost. They can be used to provide an immediate response to a disaster incident. Web-based applications can be hosted at remote locations, which will keep them safe from local disaster problems such as failed ISPs or the loss of power. A library that has a strong social media presence can detect early on if its disaster response is about to turn into a public relations disaster.

Naturally, there are some potential drawbacks to relying on free web and social medial applications.

1. It is difficult to predict the long-term viability of the application. Will this application be around a year from now when you are faced with an actual disaster?
2. Many institutions do not recommend storing personnel data (e.g., staff contact information) and other sensitive data on hosted servers or on the web.
3. Your staff must be familiar with these tools before a disaster occurs, but there can be a significant investment in time for setting up and training staff how to use a web-based or social media tool that they are not already familiar with. You may question whether this is a worthwhile use of time because disasters are infrequent.
4. Once your staff has mastered these tools, then they must keep their social media skills current and their web accounts active.

Perhaps the biggest area of concern with the use of web-based and social media tools for disaster communication is that these tools may have limited usefulness because only a small number of library patrons participate in library social media networks. In other words, unless your library has a large community of tech-savvy patrons and has established a sizable social media following, you are not going to reach many people via your online posts. If your library's Facebook page has only fifty followers, then Facebook may not be the way to get the word out about your library's temporary service hours during a disaster.

Tips for Using Web and Social Media Applications

Go where your stakeholders are. Survey the social media landscape in your community or on your campus to find out where your patrons are. It is important to pick easy-to-use applications that staff already use, or which they can learn easily, rather than those that may have steep learning curves. Host your applications at remote locations rather than on your own servers. Finally, make sure that your stakeholders are aware of your alternate communication channels.

Your Social Media Communication Tree

The Disaster Team leader should designate who will say what when disaster strikes, and account for staff whereabouts throughout the disaster. Naturally, the designated spokesperson for internal and external communication (typically the Library Director or Library Dean) will handle communication with all traditional media (print, media, radio, etc.). However, the designated spokesperson may assign other library staff the responsibility for updating the library's social media and web accounts, which may include

- library website updates
- Twitter, Facebook, and Pinterest updates
- blog and Tumblr posts
- Instagram, Vine, and YouTube images and videos
- Messages using the email traffic handler for your common library accounts (e.g., info@, reference@, or circulation@)

As part of your library's disaster communication plan, you need to make sure that your staff is trained and equipped to work remotely. In the event any one of the members of the social media communication tree cannot be contacted, make sure each role has a backup, or that others are adequately trained to pick up the slack. As you go about responding to the disaster, do not be afraid to publicize any setbacks that might occur—you may be surprised at the number of volunteers who will step up to the plate to help once they are made aware of what is going on with your library. Finally, make sure that the team issues regular status reports on where you are and what has been accomplished to make sure that you are all on the same page.

AFTER RECOVERY

After your library has successfully recovered from the disaster, make sure to thank your staff, supporters, and volunteers. Next, analyze your disaster communication plan for lessons learned and modify your plan as needed. Do not forget to market your successes, such as the reopening of building and collections and restoration of services. Use those updates to stress the importance of your library to the community that you serve.

How Ready Is Your Library?

Answer the following questions to determine if your library has an adequate communication disaster plan and is ready to respond to a disaster:

1. Do you have a disaster plan that is updated regularly? Does that plan include a communication plan or address the role of communication in a disaster?

2. Do you have a social media communication tree with backups assigned for each role?

3. Are your staff trained and equipped to work remotely?

4. Does your communication plan incorporate redundancy of communication (such as what to do if landlines and cell phones do not work)?

5. Does your plan include procedures for updating the library website and social media applications like Facebook and Twitter?

6. Is your staff trained to do situation awareness reporting? Have they practiced reporting *who, what, when,* and *where* before, during, and after a service disruption?

7. Do you complete at least one training exercise or drill per year?

8. Is your library integrated into community/parent institution's disaster communication plan?

9. Do you have regular contact with emergency planners?

10. Do you plan to do post-recovery review within seven days of a service disruption or a disaster?

Adapted from NN/LM Emergency Preparedness and Response Initiative, http://nnlm.gov/ep/2014/08/05/how-ready-is-your-library.

CONCLUSION

Disaster communication plans look good on paper, but libraries cannot rely on an ideal scenario of physical communication and social networks because they may be impacted during the disaster in ways that may impede an effective disaster response and slow down your recovery process. In disaster response, you learn to plan ahead, prepare your staff to work with the best resources available, and improvise as needed.

NOTES

1. Camila C. Alire, ed., *Library Disaster Planning and Recovery Handbook* (New York: Neal-Schuman, 2000).

2. Yi Ling Wong and Ravonne Green, "Disaster Planning in Libraries," *Journal of Access Services* 4, no. 3–4 (2006): 71–82.

3. Gregory Schmidt, "Web 2.0 for Disaster Response and Recovery," *Journal of Web Librarianship* 4, no. 4 (2010): 413–426.

4. Miriam B. Kahn, *Disaster Response and Planning for Libraries*, 3rd ed. (Chicago: ALA Editions, 2012).

RESOURCES

National Network of Libraries of Medicine, Middle Atlantic Region. Disaster Information Resources. http://nnlm.gov/mar/emergency.html.

New Jersey State Library Disaster Planning Resources. www.njstatelib.org/services_for_libraries/resources/disaster_planning.

One Page Service Continuity Plan Template. http://nnlm.gov/ep/disaster-plan -templates.

Pennsylvania State University Emergency Response Guide. https://docs.google .com/file/d/0B_G06vC6SWfGdTA3NmdZbFdRaUU/edit.

Resources Conservation Center for Art and Historic Artifacts. Mid-Atlantic Resource Guide for Disaster Preparedness. www.ccaha.org/publications/ emergency-resource-guide.

Roanoke Public Library Disaster Plan. http://roanoke.lib.in.us/policies/disaster -plan-2.

43

Chapter Five

Future Trends
Cloud Computing and Disaster Mitigation

Marshall Breeding

Cloud computing has already begun to transform the use of technology in libraries. The current phase of technology has seen a shift away from computer systems housed and maintained within the premises of a library or its parent institution toward an increasing reliance on software-as-a-service and other variants of cloud computing. This transformation offers a set of tradeoffs of benefits and challenges that must be balanced as libraries consider options in building their technology infrastructure. Cloud-based applications do not depend on local servers and may not lend themselves to the traditional daily backup routines practiced by many computer systems administrators in libraries. Applications delivered through software-as-a-service, for example, relieve library personnel from many of the complex tasks involved in maintaining local infrastructure. I see many benefits in channeling the efforts of library personnel toward higher-level tasks with more immediate impact on the library and its users. It is essential, however, to maintain at least the same thresholds of reliability and performance through any change from locally housed equipment to services accessed through cloud-computing technologies. Libraries must be vigilant to ensure that backup and data integrity procedures offer at least the same level of protection as apply with locally maintained systems. Moving to cloud computing demands carefully considered disaster response and recovery planning. This chapter discusses the key issues that should be addressed and offers some practical advice on disaster planning.

My perspective on and experience with disaster management has been accumulated through my many years of working with technology for the Vanderbilt University Libraries and in the management of the technical infrastructure of Library Technology Guides (librarytechnology.org) and other projects. While at Vanderbilt University, I was also responsible for the Vanderbilt Television News Archive (tvnews.vanderbilt.edu), which presented significant challenges in the development of contingency plans for a massive collection of more than 50,000 hours of digital video consuming at least 150 terabytes of storage. Library Technology Guides relies on infrastructure provided through hosting services for which I have developed disaster recovery and backup plans that have resulted in continuous operation for over a decade without interruption. As a consultant, I have also reviewed the technical infrastructure and disaster recovery strategies of many different organizations. This chapter is informed primarily through my three decades of practical experience and therefore does not cite scholarly resources on the topic. I hope that this practical approach can benefit other libraries as they face the intersection of cloud technology and disaster planning.

INEVITABILITY OF CLOUD TECHNOLOGIES IN LIBRARIES

Cloud computing has come to play a growing role in a library's technical infrastructure. An increasing number of new products offered to libraries are deployed via web-based platforms, hosted external to the library. The model of running software on a computer housed in the library or in the data center of its parent institution will fade.

Some examples of the types of library-oriented products offered primarily through cloud-based platforms follow.

Storage Services

Storage services are used for files shared among individual employees or collaborative projects. In addition to, or instead of, using departmental or institutional file servers or shared folders, many people use Dropbox, Google Drive, Microsoft OneDrive, or similar services.

Libraries also continue to manage other types of data on local storage devices. We work in a type of hybrid infrastructure that requires more complex strategies for disaster planning that must accommodate both approaches to data management, each of which demands different processes and procedures.

Library Services Platforms

Some of the newer generation products for managing library resources are offered exclusively through software-as-a-service, including OCLC WorldShare Management Services, Ex Libris Alma, and ProQuest Intota. Sierra, offered by Innovative Interfaces, can be deployed either as a hosted service or on locally housed servers.[1]

Integrated Library Systems

Integrated library systems (ILSs) that follow a more traditional library automation model are increasingly being offered as hosted services by vendors or support providers. The proportion of libraries opting for a vendor-hosted ILS continues to rise each year. A library that does not want to update its ILS will often opt to shift to a hosted arrangement when its current local server approaches the end of its expected life or when it experiences a major failure.

47

Discovery Services

Many of the discovery products that libraries deploy to provide access to their resources to library patrons come only as cloud-based services. Examples include BiblioCommons, ProQuest Summon, Ex Libris Primo Central, EBSCO Discovery Service, and OCLC's WorldCat Discovery Service. These discovery services, which include access to massive indexes, could not feasibly be implemented through local installations and provide an example of categories of library-oriented products that would not necessarily be possible without the advent of cloud-based technologies.

Subject Guides

Many libraries have migrated away from subject guides implemented as HTML pages on local web servers to web-based hosted services such as Springshare's LibGuides.

Email and Other Productivity Applications

These applications have also seen increased deployment through cloud platforms. Universities, for example, routinely outsource student email services to cloud-based systems from Google or Microsoft. Microsoft is making a gradual transition from versions of its Office suite of productivity applications that are installed on laptop or desktop computers to its Office 360 service, which deploys through the web.

Because so many new applications and new versions of existing applications, are being offered through cloud technologies, it will be increasingly difficult for libraries to avoid employing cloud technologies to support their critical systems. This makes it imperative for libraries to develop strategies that provide protection and control of their data, even when it is managed off-site and by external organizations.

SETTING EXPECTATIONS

An organization's strategy for disaster planning and recovery must avoid or lessen the impact of the many categories of failures that may occur throughout its technical infrastructure. The key objective of this strategy lies in ensuring that no computer-related events or failures will impair its ability to carry out its work. Experience proves that computer-based systems will never be perfect. It takes proactive efforts to minimize or mitigate the impact of inevitable failures. Some of the basic components of a disaster planning strategy apply regardless of the way in which the infrastructure is deployed, whether locally managed systems or those provided through a remote service provider.

A disaster planning and recovery strategy centers on minimizing any interruptions in service or loss of data in the event of any technology malfunctions, including those related to human error. The basic principles of disaster planning and recovery have been discussed in other chapters in this LITA Guide. This chapter focuses on the concerns that apply when libraries introduce cloud-based technologies.

When planning for the contingencies related to the services or infrastructure components provided through cloud-computing technologies, it is essential to meet or exceed the levels of protection used for locally managed hardware and software. With adequate planning and preparation, the opportunities for data loss or service interruption can be reduced as the library moves to cloud technologies, because in most cases they are based on highly redundant components that may not be practical to implement when using locally managed computer equipment.

In some scenarios, the library has more control over the application managed through cloud technologies than others. In a product like a discovery service or a library services platform delivered through software-as-a-service, all aspects of the hardware, software, and related data components are managed by the provider. In these cases, disaster planning will involve a review and negotiation of those procedures between the library and the provider to ensure that data integrity, backup, and possibilities for service interruptions are carried out within tolerances approved by the library. (These issues will be discussed in greater detail in the section below on service-level agreements.)

In other cases, the infrastructure may be based on cloud technologies, but remain under the direct control of the library. Implementation of projects or applications based on infrastructure-as-a-service can be assembled by the library, with a variety of options available to handle possible failures. In these scenarios, the options for disaster planning follow the same principles as for local hardware, and the library can create as much redundancy in hardware and software components as it can afford relative to the level of protection required and the tolerance for service interruptions.

In any cloud-computing environment, the reduction of risk is tied directly to increases in cost. The disaster strategy must balance the maximum period of allowable service interruption versus the increasing costs associated with each level of protection that can minimize that interval. Creating an environment with no redundancy represents the least expensive option. Yet, the failure of any given component can result in service interruptions that will involve a longer time to recover. Architecting an operating environment with full redundancy of all components can double its infrastructure and software costs. Although it is possible to build systems so redundant that the possibility for failure is almost eliminated, the costs may be prohibitive for libraries. In the same way that a library may not opt for replicates of the local production server for its ILS when it is housed by the library due to cost constraints, it likewise may not always opt for provisioning multiple replicates of services it operates through an infrastructure-as-a-service provider. It is often the case, however, that the cost of redundant components can be less when using infrastructure services rather than equipment acquired and managed locally.

PROTECTION OF DATA IS PARAMOUNT

For libraries and similar organizations, the priority centers on eliminating any possibility of data loss. Even in the event of a catastrophic failure, it is essential that all data and metadata related to an institution's collections, financial data, and other operational data be recoverable. It is imperative that all data be managed

49

in such a way that systems can be restored comprehensively in the event of any failure. Although the ability to reconstruct the hardware and software components of failed systems is important, that capability is moot if the data needed to bring them back to an operational state is corrupted, or if data is lost that must be manually reconstructed.

It is essential that copies of data that form the basis of restoring a system be as current as is practically possible, that they be housed in such a way that they can be accessed quickly, and that their integrity is guaranteed. Backup copies of data should be stored on media and on infrastructure entirely isolated from the primary system to ensure that they are not impacted by any failure of the production system. The data should be stored in a way that enables reasonably quick retrieval. Offline storage arrangements that may require several hours to access backup copies, for example, may cause major frustration in times of an emergency restoration. Validating the integrity of the backup copies as they are made is also essential, though often difficult to accomplish. Catastrophic failures are made even worse when it is discovered that all available backup copies have been corrupted. It is important to preserve copies of data spanning multiple backup cycles to ensure that it is possible to recover data, even if it is not necessarily the most recent copy.

CATEGORIES OF CLOUD SERVICES

The term *cloud computing* tends to be used rather loosely to describe almost any type of technology service hosted remotely. It is important, however, to understand each of the different types of offerings, their relative advantages or limitations, and the different concerns relative to disaster planning and recovery that may apply. Cloud services cover a wide range of approaches, including those that require the library to develop and execute procedures for data security to others entirely controlled by the provider, where data protection issues are addressed primarily through contractual terms.

Infrastructure-as-a-Service

This level of cloud computing provides computing components that will be managed directly by the library to manage an application. A library might manage the operation of an ILS or digital repository itself, but instead of operating it on servers housed locally, it runs them on servers in a third-party data center or other infrastructure provider. The categories of infrastructure might include basic computing and storage devices, more complex services related to network management, load balancing, database engines, or a variety of other technical services. The most popular infrastructure-as-a-service provider is Amazon, through its Elastic Compute Cloud (EC2) web service, Simple Storage Services (S3), and related offerings. Many other providers also offer similar infrastructure services.

Infrastructure-as-a-service provides the underlying components of any service or application. A wide range of scenarios apply relative to disaster planning. Projects deployed using components provisioned through these types of services provide more control and responsibility for the management of data. For those implementing projects based on infrastructure-as-a-service, the section below on designing fault-tolerant systems describes some options available to avoid or recover from component failures.

Storage-as-a-Service

This subset of infrastructure-as-a-service provides capacity for the subscriber to store data. These services range from those oriented to enterprise storage for large and complex organizations to basic storage for personal use. They come in many different forms, each with its own implications for disaster planning. Redundancy in storage technology deployed through cloud-based services can be implemented in various ways, many of them similar to those that apply to local storage equipment.

Storage services designed for large organizations offer large-scale capacity and a variety of options regarding how the storage will be managed and priced. Some of the relevant configuration options might include the manner in which data is replicated or the performance level of the storage service. The configurations with more redundancy will of course be priced higher than raw unmanaged storage.

Within any given piece of storage, arrays of drives can be assembled and configured to provide some degree of fault tolerance in order to preserve data, and to continue to function even in the event of the failure of one of the storage components. These redundant arrays of inexpensive disks (RAID) have been a standard offering in the storage-technology arena since the 1980s. The way that data is organized across the independent drives within a RAID storage device varies, with each level capable of delivering different levels of cost, reliability, or performance. RAID either physically duplicates data on multiple drives, or uses algorithms based on parity bits so that data can be reconstructed in the event of a component failure.

Although RAID-based storage systems are capable of producing very high levels of reliability, they do not protect against many categories of systematic failures. Additionally, RAID systems can fail. The hardware and software that manage a RAID-based system can fail or malfunction in ways that can induce catastrophic data loss. Some RAID systems include redundancy of supporting components such as controllers and power supplies.

Another layer of data protection involves the replication of data in separate storage services isolated from each other. This redundancy can be accomplished within the services of an infrastructure provider that offers data replication. Replication of data services within the same physical data center offers protection against many categories of failure.

Additional protection is gained when duplicate copies are made on entirely independent storage infrastructure. Many storage providers manage data centers in different geographic regions, making it possible to have well-dispersed copies and still operate within a single management environment. Some infrastructure providers may offer tools that automatically synchronize data sets between regions, with high-capacity bandwidth connecting their network of data centers that increases the speed in which replicates can be produced or retrieved, which may decrease the associated connectivity costs. Amazon, for example, offers data replication across data centers in geographic regions. Although a more expensive option, this type of replication offers continuity of services even in the event of an Internet outage or other catastrophic failure that impacts an entire data center.

Creating duplicate copies of data incurs expense, which must be taken into consideration during budget planning for any major project that will be based on cloud technologies. These costs can take the form of additional raw storage for a self-managed backup process, or for higher-tier storage options in enterprise-oriented services. When the data replicates reside in storage services from different providers, there will likely be additional connectivity costs, especially if the data sets are quite large.

In the realm of small data sets, the costs of cloud-based storage can be minimal, or even free. There are many services oriented to individual use that offer free storage up to a set threshold. These free services have become extremely popular, but must be approached skeptically from a disaster planning perspective. They can be convenient to use, with software or drivers that emulate a local storage device that require no additional effort to save data beyond the familiar procedures.

Storage services usually offer no guarantees or liability for the provider in the event of data loss. It is essential to never rely completely on any given storage service, just like one would never depend on any given local hard drive to store important data. Cloud services tend to be quite reliable, which may instill a sense of false confidence. No disaster and recovery plan should tolerate data on a single storage service or device.

It is possible, however, to develop a tenable data-management strategy for projects involving small data sets, or for personal or professional use, based on free storage services. Such a strategy would involve working with multiple services, usually in combination with copies that reside on local hardware.

Keep in mind that data stored on local drives, especially on portable devices, should be considered the most vulnerable storage option. Files on these devices can be lost in the event of equipment failure, but theft or loss of the device itself presents the greatest concern. Although it is often necessary to keep working files on an individual laptop or desktop computer, much greater security and protection can be achieved through either the institutional network or through a cloud-based storage service.

Depending on logistical considerations, the primary working copy of data files might reside on local hardware or in a cloud-storage service. If the project is carried out in an environment with persistent Internet connectivity, it may be possible for primary working copies to reside in a remote storage service. Other projects may take place where connectivity is less reliable. In these cases, working copies of files would reside on local drives, which can be synchronized to cloud services.

In order to use personal cloud storage services safely, it is important to take additional measures to create duplicate copies stored on different services or local media. A variety of utilities are available that synchronize data across multiple storage services, such as CloudHQ (www.cloudhq.net). An alternate approach might involve creating scripts or other automated processes that can be activated periodically through the system-scheduling utility of a personal computer to copy or synchronize data across service providers. Regardless of the approach taken, it is important to frequently inspect files and folders to be sure that they have been distributed as expected.

Vendor-Hosted Instances

One flavor of cloud computing, often marketed as software-as-a-service, takes the form of a provider hosting a server-based application. Applications developed when client-server architectures prevailed were designed to be deployed on server platforms dedicated for each implementation. In the ILS realm, an instance might

53

support either a single library or a consortium composed of many libraries and branches. These instances scale to quite extensive implementation scenarios, often using clusters of multiple servers for hardware support. Individual servers might be allocated to house the database, web service, and the software application itself. Each implementation operates entirely independently of those of other organizations that use the same software. As early as the 1990s, some ILS vendors offered a hosted version of their products under what was known as an application service provider arrangement. These services have grown increasingly popular, and have generally been marketed in recent years as software-as-a-service.

In this type of hosting arrangement, use of the system takes place through client software configured to communicate with the server component housed by the service provider. The clients related to staff-oriented functions may be implemented as software installed on desktop operating systems such as Microsoft Windows or the Macintosh OS, or implemented in Java. Web-based clients are becoming increasingly common.

In the ILS arena, staff-oriented clients have traditionally been implemented for Windows or Java with end-user access provided through web-based applications. In recent years, there has been considerable development in redeveloping staff interfaces to operate through a web browser. Even as these products shift to fully web-based interfaces, the server component may continue to follow an architecture where a separate instance of the software is dedicated to each institution or implementation.

The disaster recovery procedures for an instance of the software hosted by a vendor remain the same as if the software was installed within the library's data center. The important difference is that the responsibility to execute the disaster mitigation procedures shifts to the provider instead of the library. The standard components of the strategy include:

- All operational data must be backed up as frequently as possible.
- Transaction logs should be available to complete the restoration of data created or altered since the last reliable backup.
- Backups should be regularly validated.
- Backup sets across multiple cycles should be saved.
- Backup sets should be saved in off-site locations.
- Restoration procedures should be tested.

Vendors that host multiple instances are often ideally positioned to manage disaster planning and recovery. Those that manage hundreds or thousands of instances of an application will likely have sophisticated tools that control the deployment of instances and have enterprise-quality backup systems and procedures to protect customer data. The provider, for example, may have instances of the software at the ready that can be quickly configured for a customer site and populated with data from backup media in the event of a failure.

Vendors that deploy their products through software-as-a-service operate at a scale that offers efficiencies that are not available to a library operating a single instance of the system. To operate these large data centers in a responsible way, these providers employ specialists devoted to each operational area, including system security and disaster planning. It is rare, in contrast, for a library to be able to dedicate one or more technical personnel to data security and disaster planning.

The downside of relying on a vendor that provides its products through large-scale hosting services lies in the risk of widespread failure. Though the chances for a failure may be drastically decreased through the levels of security and redundancy that would be implemented in a large-scale data center, any outages that occur may impact multiple libraries that rely on the system. Internet connectivity interruptions to a data center or massive, distributed denial of service attacks can disrupt access to the service to a large number of users. Such a widespread failure is also likely to attract attention that could decrease confidence in the reliability of cloud-based services. Failures that affect individual installations of systems in libraries tend not to draw public attention. Therefore the relative risks of local infrastructure versus cloud computing can be hard to evaluate.

Software-as-a-Service

The more modern form of software-as-a-service is designed as a platform that provides its functionality to multiple institutional or individual uses through a single instance. Often referred to as "multi-tenant SaaS," these platforms are designed as native web applications that rely on a single code base, and aggregate or segregate data as needed. This architecture contrasts with the application service provider arrangement, where each installation is supported through a separate instance of the software. Examples of multi-tenant platforms include social networks such as Facebook, and applications such as Gmail, Google Docs, and the other Google productivity applications. For sales and commerce, Salesforce.com is the classic example of business infrastructure delivered through a multi-tenant platform. In the library arena, multi-tenant platforms include OCLC WorldShare Management Services, Ex Libris Alma, and ProQuest Intota, as well as such major discovery services as ProQuest Summon, Ex Libris Primo Central, EBSCO Discovery Service, and BiblioCommons.

When deployed through a single code-base, new versions of the software or bug fixes can take effect for all users of the system all at once. In contrast, locally installed software requires each institution or individual to download and install a new version in order to take advantage of any new programming. Deploying new versions of software for a locally installed application is a source of continual disruption.

Almost any new product or service developed in recent years uses this multi-tenant architecture. Products previously created under client-server architecture can be re-engineered for deployment as multi-tenant applications, but this transition can be quite challenging. Many of the client-server applications in the library realm are evolving toward a multi-tenant architecture gradually; some of the initial steps include transitioning from interfaces created for desktop operating systems to ones that operate entirely through a web browser.

Multi-tenant systems manage data in fundamentally different ways than those oriented toward deployment on a server. Within a server-oriented application, because the data associated with the organization served by any given installation is held in its various data structures, a disaster response plan can employ traditional backup procedures. In contrast, in a typical multi-tenant SaaS deployment, data related to each institution's use of the service may not be managed discretely from that of other sites that use the system. Configuration options and access privileges enforce controls to ensure that users from one site may not access data related to other sites. Segregating data from an operational perspective does not necessarily mean that it is segregated relative to the lower-level data stores.

Multi-tenant applications require an entirely different set of concepts and procedures for disaster planning and recovery. In a multi-tenant platform, the provider is responsible for most, if not all, data management for all the users of the service The backup procedures will apply to the data structures for all the institutional or individual users of the system as a whole. There may or may not be procedures that routinely create separate backup sets for each institution that makes use of the platform. Access to data must take place through the client or console provided, which operates through the business logic and permissions layers that segregate customer data.

In the realm of multi-tenant platforms, the emphasis for the users centers on higher-level deliverables such as functionality, performance, and reliability. It is not necessary for a user of the system to be aware of the underlying hardware or software components. Even programmers that access the system via application program interfaces (APIs) will not need to interact with lower-level infrastructure. Service providers may make changes to the technical components that support the platform over time to enhance performance and scalability or to add new capabilities. The users of such a platform do not necessarily need to be aware of the details involved with each of the changes that are implemented as part of the routine maintenance and ongoing development of the platform. Those used to managing their own systems may find the focus on higher-level functionality without knowledge or control of low-level technical troubling, but it is a fundamental characteristic of multi-tenant software-as-a-service platforms.

In this vein, multi-tenant platforms generally do not allow end users to have access to its lower-level databases or operating system. Because these platforms support many institutions or individuals simultaneously, providing root-level access to server components or even access via SQL commands to the native databases usually cannot be allowed because this could give access to the data of other tenants. Instead, the provider of the service may provide APIs or other utilities that have been programmed to make use of the security layers that enforce data segregation. Using the provided utilities, it may be possible for any institutional user to extract data sets that resemble a system backup periodically. Because the platform as a whole is not under the control of any given institution, the usual processes for recovering or restoring a system do not apply.

Backup-as-a-Service

An infrastructure provider may include an additional set of services for system backups. Some may be comprehensive services that address all aspects of a server and will recover the entire server, including any installed software in the event of a catastrophic failure. Other services may be more limited and address only specific data components or may provide only for a restoration of the server hardware and operating system. It is essential to understand what data-protection services are provided by default, which ones are available only at premium service levels, and which tasks might need to be contracted through a third party or handled manually.

Services are available from specialized providers for the backup and restoration of systems and data. These can protect data on servers managed through cloud-based infrastructure or those housed on the premises. Most function through the installation of drivers and scheduling utilities, which activate standard backup procedures that save data within their own secure cloud storage. Such services come with a range of options, from backing up specified data files and folders to entire server and systems backup and restoration. Pricing tiers range from low-cost options for personal computers to more expensive options for servers or other enterprise-level components. Examples of these backup services include Carbonite (www.carbonite .com); CrashPlan (www.code42.com/crashplan), offered by Code42 Software; and Mozy (mozy.com), offered by the EMC, an enterprise storage provider.

Such backup services can provide a comprehensive set of tasks that can fulfill many of an organization's disaster planning and recovery requirements. Such a service can be especially beneficial to organizations that may not have technical personnel trained to implement backup procedures. Yet these services must also be carefully scrutinized to carefully understand any limitations or lapses. Some libraries may opt to use a backup service to supplement their own measures to increase the level of protection to their data.

DESIGNING FAULT-TOLERANT SYSTEMS

One of the key aspects of a disaster planning strategy is the implementation of measures to decrease the possibility that the system might experience a failure. Systems should be designed to be fault-tolerant, making it necessary to rebuild and restore only in rare scenarios. In the event of a failure, fault-tolerant systems can also continue to function with degraded capacity, or standby systems can be activated promptly. The ability to recover from a failure can be strengthened through a variety of means, most of which are related to replication of services and equipment. With enough redundancy, the possibility of an interruption in service becomes almost nonexistent. But should a failure occur, the organization needs to be able to bring its systems back online as quickly as possible. A range of approaches are available in the cloud-computing sphere to achieve increasing levels of survivability despite failures, each with its associated costs.

Active Redundancy

Active redundancy can almost eliminate the impact of a failure—even of an entire server. In this configuration, all hardware and software components of a platform are replicated and configured to participate in its ongoing operation. Such a configuration can increase the performance capability during peak periods because multiple processors, database servers, and other components are available to service requests. In the event of a failure, the remaining components can continue to function, although the system as a whole may experience diminished performance. This type of active redundancy can be implemented through hardware- and software-management utilities that enable hardware and software components to function as a cluster. Careful attention must be paid to ensure that database transactions or other sensitive operations function correctly when being updated by multiple sources.

Database Clustering

The implementation of database-management systems to support an application can be designed to increase reliability and protect against some categories of data loss. A database-driven application can be designed to take advantage of clustered configurations where multiple instances of the database operate across independent hardware platforms. Operating in a synchronized or master/slave relationship, a clustered database implementation effectively increases operational reliability and can dramatically improve the performance of the application at the same time. If one of the clusters becomes unavailable, the application continues to function with the support of the remaining database replicates. Clustering can also be used to minimize or eliminate service interruptions that might otherwise be required when creating routine backups of the database. One replicate can be temporarily removed from the cluster so that its copy of the database can be the basis for the backup, and resynchronized upon completion.

Transaction Logging

Transaction logging adds a layer of protection through its ability to recover database transactions that may have transpired between a system failure and the last valid backup. Many enterprise-level applications have been programmed to manage interactions with the underlying database to provide a log of relevant transactions. The transaction log can then be processed following a system failure so that it essentially plays back the transactions that transpired from the time of the last backup.

Proactive measures related to transaction logging would include determining whether or not any given service or application offers this capability, ensuring that it is activated, directing transaction logs to a separate file system from the application itself, and documenting procedures needed to access and process the transaction log in the event that a system restoration is needed.

Standby Systems

Organizations may also have a copy of a system that is available to be switched to production use whenever needed, although this is less reliable than the redundant clustered components described above. It is common, for example, for a library to operate a "test server" for its ILS or other major systems to validate new software releases, test local scripts or programs, and perform related purposes. Because it is used for risky operations, a test server remains isolated from the production environment. But when the production system fails, the test system can be refreshed quickly with the current data and placed into operational use. For a test server to have the capability to stand in for the production server, it must be sized accordingly. The use of standby servers functions in much the same way for both local equipment and infrastructure provisioned through cloud services.

Reserved Instances

Cloud infrastructure, such as the Amazon Elastic Compute Cloud (http://aws.amazon.com/ec2), offers capabilities to reserve instances of any given platform that remain dormant until activated. Such a reserved instance can be preconfigured with the necessary processor, memory, and storage, as well as database and other software components. In most cases, an instance of a set of components can be configured and left idle with no ongoing costs. But, when needed, that reserved instance can be activated and placed into production quickly, without the delay that would result from provisioning and configuring instances and loading software components at the time of a failure. This kind of standby capability applies only to cloud-based infrastructure services and has no real equivalent in the realm of local computing.

In general, cloud-based technologies offer a wide range of options to implement levels of redundancy that would not be possible or practical otherwise. With local equipment, the time to recovery can be lengthened by the need to procure failed hardware components. Provisioning computing resources through an infrastructure service can be done in minutes, in contrast to the much longer process of procurement, delivery, installation, and configuration needed for locally deployed equipment.

SERVICE-LEVEL AGREEMENTS

In the realm of multi-tenant software-as-a-service platforms, the processes and procedures related to disaster planning and recovery are carried out by the provider.

Institutions that rely on these kinds of platforms for critical functions do not simply assume that these procedures will be followed. Rather, when a library contracts or subscribes to one of these services, it should require documentation of the backup and other disaster recovery procedures in place, be aware of any certifications that the institution or its data center have earned in data-management practices, and have a service-level agreement that describes the levels of availability, performance, and other expectations in quantifiable terms.

When engaging with services provided through software-as-a-service, a service-level agreement defines the terms in which that service will be provided and supported. Especially for multi-tenant platforms, the library itself cannot directly carry out the tasks that ensure the protection of data or other activities related to disaster planning and recovery. To even consider adopting such a service, the library needs to have confidence that the service will be reliable and highly available as well as meet its functional requirements. In a community as well connected as libraries, the reputation of platform as either stable or reliable or as one with a high frequency of downtime or other issues will likely become known through informal channels. But when considering strategic technology products, it is essential to base decisions on objective performance data and by the terms specified in a service-level agreement.

The service-level agreement will specify the expectations for service delivery. Terms will address the tolerable levels of service interruption, the speed at which the system will respond to each transaction or request, and other measures of operational performance. The agreement might state, for example, the percentage of time during the service period for which the service will be unavailable. The service-level agreement will also specify any penalties that might be assessed by the institution when service falls below the stated thresholds. The agreement may also define limits of liability and how disputes related to the service will be resolved.

The service-level agreement will not necessarily specify the manner in which the system will be operated. As part of the procurement process, the service provider may disclose many of the details of the technical components that support the platform and the procedures used in data management and security. Libraries should not expect service-level agreements to specify the details of internal procedures the provider follows, but rather the guaranteed performance levels. Technical details may provide evidence to help an organization gain confidence that these benchmarks will be met, but are generally not part of the final contract.

Providers of cloud-based platforms may also earn certifications that validate that they meet industry standards in certain areas. The certifications that carry the most weight are those given by international industry groups with rigorous validation processes. The certifications that apply to data centers relative to data security include:

- ISO/IEC 27001:2005: Information technology—Security techniques— Information security management systems—Requirements (www.iso .org/iso/catalogue_detail?csnumber=42103). Although now superseded, many data centers and providers continue to assert this certification as they seek certification under the new version.
- ISO/IEC 27001:2013: Information technology—Security techniques— Information security management systems—Requirements (www .iso.org/iso/home/store/catalogue_ics/catalogue_detail_ics.htm? csnumber=54534).
- SAS 70 (Statement on Auditing Standards No. 70): Developed by the American Institute of Certified Accountants, addresses the controls in place regarding information technology systems that handle financial information; to claim this certification, the data center must pass an audit carried out by an independent certified public accounting firm (www.sas70.com).

Other certifications address overall quality performance of the service provider (ISO 9001) and controls in place to reduce environmental impact (ISO 14001).

Note that many of the providers of applications delivered through software-as-a-service do not manage their own data centers, but rely on infrastructure components housed in data centers of third-party providers. The overall reliability of the service depends on both the software components and technical architecture developed by the service provider and the low-level infrastructure that may be provided through a third party. Working with third-party infrastructure providers gives software developers access to highly scalable resources and globally distributed data centers.

DATA OWNERSHIP

Another important issue to be addressed with multi-tenant platforms is data ownership. Libraries need to be clear regarding the rights that they have to any data that they use or create on that platform. In a server-oriented system, data ownership issues are better defined, because each instance is dedicated to a particular library or consortium. With multi-tenant platforms, data is more widely shared and inter-mingled among the many different subscribing organizations. For systems with a shared bibliographic database, for example, no single institution may have exclusive ownership of any given record. An important consideration concerns the ability to withdraw from the use of an incumbent system and move to another, with the legal right and technical means to transfer any relevant data.

From an operational perspective, shared data provides considerable efficiency. Shared knowledge bases of bibliographic data or e-journal holdings can save librar-ies from the burden of maintaining these resources independently. But as libraries participate in shared data resources, it is also important to track the data that rep-resents a library's collection and operations. Libraries may at some point need to change to another system and require the ability to migrate their data accordingly.

These issues must be addressed in any contract that the library executes for a platform that supports an aspect of its critical operations. Any contract for use of a cloud-based platform should include terms that specify ownership or intellectual property rights regarding each category of data and whether the library is entitled to extract data for backup purposes or upon terminating use of the service. A library might, for example, expect terms such as the right to receive a copy of each bibliographic record to which it attaches items or holdings, as well as transactional data related to acquisitions, circulation, and other applicable operational areas.

IMPACT ON PERSONNEL

A shift to cloud computing essentially outsources much of the work related to the lower-level technical infrastructure for library-related applications. The technical personnel in the library no longer need to attend to the maintenance of server hardware, operating systems, or the technical operation of the software.

Libraries that rely primarily on applications delivered through cloud-computing technologies will need fewer personnel on staff trained in server hardware platforms or systems administration of operating systems. Those libraries that do not have personnel trained in systems administration or other skills related to low-level computing infrastructure find cloud-based services a good fit.

An increased reliance on cloud technologies does not mean that a library cannot make use of personnel with technology skills. An environment where the library manages systems, but relies more on cloud-based infrastructure than local equipment, requires similar levels of technical expertise. For those institutions implementing provider-managed systems through software-as-a-service, the emphasis of technology skills shifts upward from focusing on low-level infrastructure to working with the applications at a more functional level. The basic administration of applications delivered through software-as-a-service is not generally a technical task, where configuration options are managed through a web-based console. Such a configuration requires an understanding of the nuances of the application and the benefits or consequences of each configuration option, but does not necessarily require knowledge of the underlying technical details.

One of the key opportunities for technologists in the area of cloud computing lies in working with the APIs of the various services to create scripts or applications that enable multiple systems to work together well, exchange data without need for duplicate effort, and create new snippets of functionality to fill in the gaps not addressed by the services as delivered.

The shift in technical personnel toward higher-level work may also mean eliminating staff positions for the systems administrators that have traditionally been responsible for disaster planning, backups, and recovery. The operational use of applications delivered through software-as-a-service may not require staff trained to manage low-level infrastructure. Nonetheless, it will still be necessary to perform technical reviews of how these applications manage the library's critical data stores and to ensure that there are adequate processes and procedures that meet the requirements of the library's disaster planning strategy.

The technical review of the data-management processes should be performed under the supervision of the library. The vendor will need to provide documentation of the processes under its control, but it is also important to have independent verification of these procedures. In libraries involved with multiple cloud-based services, each would have its own review.

It is essential to coordinate disaster planning across all the systems and services on which the library relies, including both local and cloud-based services. The backup data sets from multiple services, how they are transferred among providers and media, the versions retained, and other details must be coordinated and managed to avoid lapses and confusion. Some libraries may choose to target backup copies onto a cloud-based storage provider or to locally managed storage media. Any replicates of data among storage services and local media should also be managed to operate automatically, make efficient use of the storage available, and clearly label the source and time of capture. Backup operations that operate without human intervention are less likely to have lapses. It will still be important for these tasks to be reviewed periodically to confirm that they continue to operate as designed. All backup operations should generate messages to notify the appropriate library personnel upon completion or to have other mechanisms to ensure that any failure is evident and can be immediately rectified.

WORKING WITHIN INSTITUTIONAL POLICIES AND PRACTICES

Most organizations have set policies and procedures regarding the storage of institutional data. Some provide enterprise storage accessed via a network allocated to departments, workgroups, projects, and individual employees. These enterprise storage environments are usually managed by a central information technology department and will follow standard practices related to disaster planning. Some libraries, especially larger ones, may manage their own network storage environments.

This chapter does not address disaster planning for enterprise infrastructure managed within an organization. It is critical to ensure that any cloud-based storage services are implemented in ways that do not negate the capabilities of these environments to provide secure data storage. Many organizations require that work-related data be stored only within their managed infrastructures, and therefore may prohibit sensitive, or even routine, data to be placed on external services. When considering the use of cloud-based storage services, it is important to comply with any such institutional policies or mandates.

Some organizations, especially those financed with public funds, may be required to manage their data in ways that ensure its availability to the public records regulations. Dispersing data through multiple cloud-storage services makes it difficult for an organization to perform mandated accountability and records-management activities.

AVOID DATA CHAOS

Keeping data files properly organized can be an important part of a data-management strategy. Many professionals work with data files related to diverse activities; these may be directly related to their primary work position, to workgroups that extend beyond that organization, and to personal projects.

65

It is easy for data files to fall into chaotic disarray. Some may be stored within the institutional network, others remain on the local drive of a desktop or laptop computer, and others on cloud-based services. A disaster planning and recovery strategy cannot protect files that reside outside of its managed infrastructure.

PRIVACY AND CONFIDENTIALITY

Another consideration with any cloud-based service concerns confidentiality, privacy, and who has access to personal or institutional data. It is essential to have clarity regarding these critical questions. Do the terms of service or service agreement allow the provider to scan and make use of the content of the data in any way? Under what circumstances will the provider make data available to law enforcement authorities? What security measures are in place to ensure that data cannot be compromised and accessed through malicious attacks? Each of these issues should be clearly specified in the subscription agreement or the contract that governs the service.

CONNECTIVITY IS KING

One of the key areas of concern as an organization moves to cloud-based infrastructure relates to the reliability of Internet connectivity. As organizations increasingly rely on cloud technologies, business continuity depends on connectivity to the Internet. Lapses in connectivity—even when the services or platforms themselves are functioning properly—can result in interruptions to critical systems that disrupt the work of the organization and may impact access of the services it provides to its clientele.

Internet connectivity must provide adequate capacity, reliability, and security. A shift to cloud-based infrastructure will mean that much of the traffic that flowed within the library's internal network must now pass through its Internet connection. Detailed capacity planning must be carried out to ensure that the organization subscribes to adequate bandwidth to provide fast performance even during peak periods.

Network traffic patterns change drastically as a library system shifts from a locally housed server to one hosted by a provider and accessed via the Internet. A library system that serves branches distributed across a particular geographic area and which houses its own server would need to optimize connectivity between those branches and the central facility that housed the server. Many municipal or public library systems might operate dedicated networks or implement wide-area network links to support this configuration. When the server is hosted by a provider, all of the facilities then rely on their connections to the Internet. These connections may continue to route through the network provided by the library, or they may instead rely on commodity Internet connections. Library systems that include facilities in rural areas with limited options for Internet connectivity may need to pay special attention to connectivity-oriented capacity planning.

The reliability of connectivity, like any category of infrastructure, can be greatly enhanced through redundancy. Having multiple Internet connections deployed by different providers can increase operational capacity and ensure availability at reduced levels in the case of an outage. As libraries and other organizations make increased use of cloud technologies, it is essential to invest in appropriate levels of Internet connectivity.

NETWORK SECURITY

Cloud-based services also invoke issues related to network security. Traffic related to staff functions that are otherwise contained within the library's internal network will traverse the Internet instead. Any private or sensitive information must be protected through encryption. Although this traffic should likewise be protected on local networks, the exposure from passing through the public Internet heightens concerns about privacy and security. In some cases, encryption may need to be provided through virtual private networking technologies that provide an end-to-end encrypted channel between staff computers and the remote servers. Encryption may also be built into the service. A web-based library services platform should be designed that will communicate exclusively through secured SSL connections or will invoke SSL for any activities that involve sensitive information.

CONCLUDING OBSERVATIONS

Cloud-computing technologies have an ever-expanding role in the strategic infra-structure of libraries. The tools that they use to describe and manage collections, and the delivery of content products are increasingly deployed using some flavor of cloud-based infrastructure. Many of the concepts and procedures regarding disaster planning and recovery were conceived for computing components installed onsite in the library or its parent organization's data center—and therefore under full control of an institution's personnel. Cloud computing can dramatically change these traditional arrangements.

For the intermediate future, libraries can expect to function in an environment where some of their computing infrastructure remains under their direct control and where other parts are managed more indirectly through services provided by external organizations. This chapter has attempted to highlight the issues related to disaster planning that apply to each of the different options along the spectrum between local equipment and multi-tenant software-as-a-service platforms.

Although computer components and services today have become immensely more reliable compared to what I encountered in the early years of my career, libraries must remain vigilant against any contingency that might lead to data loss or service interruption. The scenarios addressed in this chapter should not necessarily be considered definitive or comprehensive. The range of options for adopting technology is constantly in flux, and new issues and concerns regarding how to protect data will continue to emerge. My main objective in this chapter has been to emphasize the importance of taking all reasonable measures to protect data, and to spark thinking and action among those responsible for library technology infrastructure to ensure that they never have to face the loss of an organization's most important asset—data.

NOTE

1. Marshall Breeding, "Library Systems Report 2014: Competition and Strategic Cooperation," *American Libraries* 45, no. 5 (2014): 21–33.

RESOURCES

Breeding, Marshall. "Shifting to the Cloud: Reshaping Library Technology Infrastructure." *Computers in Libraries* 34, no. 2 (2014): 17–19.

——."Digital Archiving in the Age of Cloud Computing." *Computers in Libraries* 33, no. 2 (2013): 24–26.

——. "From Disaster Recovery to Digital Preservation." *Computers in Libraries* 32, no. 4 (2012): 22–24.

——. *Cloud Computing for Libraries*. Chicago: ALA TechSource, 2012.

International Standards Organization. www.iso.org.

Mitchell, Eric T. *Cloud-Based Services for Your Library: A LITA Guide*. Chicago: American Library Association, 2013.

Robinson, Glen, Ianni Vamvadelis, and Attila Narin. "Using Amazon Web Services for Disaster Recovery." January 2012. http://d36cz9buwru1tt .cloudfront.net/AWS_Disaster_Recovery.pdf.

SAS 70 (Statement on Auditing Standards No. 70). www.sas70.com.

Schmidt, Gregory. "Harnessing Web 2.0 and Cloud Computing in the Service of Disaster Response and Recovery." Paper presented at the 2011 ACRL Conference, Philadelphia, PA, March 30–April 2, 2011. www.ala.org/acrl/ sites/ala.org.acrl/files/content/conferences/confsandpreconfs/national/2011/ papers/harnessing_web2.0.pdf.

Wale, Carla P. "Cloudy with a Chance of Open Source: Open Source Integrated Library Systems and Cloud Computing in Academic Law Libraries." *Legal Reference Services Quarterly* 20, no. 4 (2011): 310–331.

Zissis, Dimitros, and Dimitrios Lekkas. "Addressing Cloud Computing Security Issues." *Future Generation Computer Systems* 28, no. 3 (2012): 583–592.

69

2

■ PART 2 ■

Managing Techmageddon: Disaster Mitigation and Lessons Learned

Chapter Six

The University of Iowa and the Flood of 2008
A Case Study

Paul A. Soderdahl

Tuesday, May 28, 2013. "The University of Iowa is taking a number of precautionary measures to prepare for potential flooding as the area copes with prolonged rainfall. A media briefing is scheduled for 4:30 p.m. Tuesday."[1]

Nearly five years after the devastating flood of 2008, officials at The University of Iowa mobilized the critical incident management team and dusted off the flood emergency response plan, a now-familiar supplement to the university's overall critical incident management plan. Back in the summer of 1993, the emergency spillway at the Coralville Dam, nine miles upstream from campus, was breached for the first time. The University of Iowa, which suffered $6 million in damages from this "100-year flood," developed a response plan to guide emergency decision-making in future floods.[2] Fifteen years later, in the summer of 2008, the spillway was breached again. University officials followed the flood response plan, but the Iowa River rose to unprecedented levels never contemplated in the original plan. This "500-year flood" came at an exponentially greater cost of $743 million.[3] Capital improvements were made throughout campus to mitigate against future flood damage, and the flood response plan was significantly updated.

The revised plan was finalized in February 2012, just in time to guide the coordinated response when the river quickly rose the following May.[4] On Tuesday, the day after Memorial Day, the water rose high enough to trigger the first set of action items for the main library and several other campus buildings. By Thursday, efforts were underway to remove books from the lowest shelves. On Friday, the art library—located on the opposite bank of the river—was shuttered because the new removable flood wall, engineered after the 2008 flood, blocked all access to and from the building. Experts predicted the spillway would be breached a third time. Fortunately, several days of unexpectedly dry weather soon followed and the river, though still well above flood stage, caused little damage to university property.

For library IT staff, the devastating 2008 flood was an unwelcome test of a four-month–old library IT disaster response plan. Five years later, the 2013 scare offered an opportunity to see if the lessons learned from 2008 were on point.

This case study will detail the long process involved in drafting the library IT disaster response plan, details of how the plan was executed during the flood of 2008, the success of new strategies to mitigate risk, lessons learned in 2008, and observations from 2013.

DRAFTING THE PLAN

Every organization recognizes the need for an IT disaster response plan that articulates priorities, enables quick decision-making during a crisis, details requirements for continuity of service, and guides recovery efforts. Putting pen to paper, however, is a daunting task.

Outside of the IT realm, a typical library has endured decades of small and large crises that impact library operations and put the physical collections at risk. Libraries have created whole departments around continuity of service (circulation) and risk mitigation (preservation). It is no wonder, then, that libraries typically have mature plans at the ready for crises affecting the physical collection. By comparison, a library IT disaster response plan is a nascent document.

The university's 2004 enterprise-wide IT disaster plan was more of a call to action than a plan of action. The document stated that "each unit must produce and maintain a Disaster Recovery Plan in order to be prepared to continue doing business in the event of a severe disruption or disaster. The focus of the plan is on actions needed to restore services and necessary operations in the event of a loss of critical functions."[5] In early 2005, a library task force was charged to develop a departmental plan accomplishing the following:

- Establish the criteria and severity of a disruption based on the impact it will have on the library's critical IT functions.

- Determine what the critical IT functions and systems are and the associated time frames for recovery.
- Determine the resources needed to support the critical IT functions and systems, and define the requirements for a recovery site.
- Identify the people, skills, resources, and supplies necessary to assist in the recovery process.
- Identify the library's vital institutional data, which must be stored off-site to support resumption of business operation.
- Document the appropriate procedures and information required for recovery.
- Provide for periodic review and updating of the plan to keep it current.
- Provide for testing of the documented procedures to ensure that they are complete and accurate.

The task force decided that a logical first step would be for each department to generate a list of its business functions. In turn, for each business function, department managers were instructed to answer the following:

1. What technology does the department use to perform this function? Are there dependencies on other technology (e.g., email functionality)?
2. Is the function mission-critical for the department, or can the department remain open for business during an outage? If the business function is mission-critical for the department, will the library need to shut down if the department cannot perform this function? If the department can remain open for business, what will be the impact on workflows?

Though well-intended, the goal of creating a comprehensive inventory proved overwhelming, and compliance was low. Within months, the project stalled and was tabled indefinitely.

Over the next year, several new campus-wide IT policies were developed or significantly revised, including a new enterprise backup and recovery policy and an institutional data-access policy. In addition, the university's internal audit department conducted a risk assessment that spanned all university business operations, which listed thirteen recommendations pertaining to IT. After months of wrestling with overlapping compliance requirements, a new task force was charged with a more narrowly defined goal: to self-audit library operations for compliance with new campus recommendations and policies. The task force quickly decided that four documents should be drafted:

1. Safe Computing Policy and Practice
2. University IT Policies and Impact on Library Staff
3. Library Data Retention Schedule
4. Library IT Disaster Recovery Plan

Progress was slow but steady. The first two documents were drafted relatively quickly, but the data retention schedule and the disaster recovery plan took considerably longer.

Because prior attempts to identify the criticality of services had always stalled when units resisted labeling any of their own functions as non-essential, there was not enough guidance for the IT team on how to prioritize actions. The solution to this logjam was to avoid wasting time and energy on making fine distinctions that would be unimportant in a real-life catastrophe.

Levels of criticality were defined as: (i) critical to university operations, (ii) critical to library operations, (iii) essential, and (iv) necessary, desirable, or non-essential. By clustering necessary, desirable, and non-essential designations, the task force reduced any anxiety participants might experience by having to labeling anything as non-essential, and embraced the reality that not all indispensable services are equally indispensable. Furthermore, services that fell under the cluster of "necessary, desirable, or non-essential" were not even inventoried. Volatile details such as vendor contacts and hardware and software lists were incorporated only by reference to minimize confusion from out-of-date information.

The resulting document focused on roles and responsibilities and strategies for receiving and disseminating accurate information during a crisis. Sections focused on identifying who would be responsible for convening the disaster response team, sending and receiving emergency communications, implementing services at a remote location, and communicating with both library staff and external constituencies. The plan was completed in February 2008, posted for comments in March, and finalized in April. In an unlikely turn of events, it was put to the test just two months later.

EXECUTING THE PLAN

Implementation of the plan can be easily divided into three distinct stages: evacuation, temporary relocation, and resuming normal operations.

Evacuation

During the week of June 9 through 13, 2008, the plan was invoked, the team assembled, and emergency steps taken to escape from the rising waters.

Monday, June 9, 2008. Campus officials decided to evacuate the low-lying arts campus, including the art and music libraries. Library staff and essential resources (e.g., course reserves) were moved from those two libraries on the west bank to the presumed safety of the main library on the higher elevation of the east side. Because both the art and music libraries were on upper floors of their respective buildings, there was almost no risk of flood water damaging the collections, but any resources left behind might be inaccessible for an extended period. Library management began to assess the risk to the main library, but the likelihood of evacuation was very low. Engineers projected flooding at the same level as in 1993, which would not put the main library building at risk. Library IT staff met to discuss worst-case scenarios. For the most part, library employees responded to the campus call for volunteers to sandbag areas considered to be at risk.

Tuesday, June 10, 2008. Library special collections and archives staff decided to move any materials sitting on the floor in the basement to higher ground. Library IT staff identified in broad terms what preventative steps to take in the unlikely event library IT services needed to be relocated.

Wednesday, June 11, 2008. The evacuation of the arts campus was complete. Art and music library staff settled into temporary quarters in the main library. No additional library resources appeared to be at risk.

Thursday, June 12, 2008. Early in the day, university officials announced that any valuable materials in twelve more buildings, including the main library, should be moved to higher ground. By mid-morning, library administrators issued the call to clear the lowest shelves in the basement, and by mid-afternoon additional shelves were added to the list. At the end of the day, campus officials indicated their intent to evacuate the main library in two days.

The library IT disaster plan was invoked and the response team was identified. The team's initial communication to library administration stated that "our expected worst-case scenario from a library IT perspective is this: Main Library building is without utilities for an extended period of time, but the campus as a whole remains operational."[6]

This was certainly not the worst case from a campus perspective; however, under certain circumstances it could become the worst case for library IT. If the overall situation on campus became truly catastrophic, problems would be so widespread that other infrastructural contingency plans would take over, giving the library IT disaster response team more time to reassess the situation. If, however, the campus remained operational and classes and research activities continued while the main library was out of commission, the technology needs would fall chiefly on library IT.

In order to prepare for this projected worst-case scenario, services in the top tier (critical to university operations) were copied from a virtual server environment to two physical servers. These two servers were relocated to the College of Engineering's data center where they could be brought online if the situation deteriorated. Arrangements were made with campus network engineers for an emergency VPN that could route the library's IP subnet to the engineering building so that vendors' IP-based authentication would be preserved. Preparations were substantially completed by the end of Thursday, and a cutover could take place any time as needed.

Friday, June 13, 2008. The situation on campus deteriorated quickly after another night of severe weather. Teams of volunteers—including students and staff, townspeople, members of the local Amish community, and prisoners on release programs—descended on the main library. They sandbagged the building's perimeter and formed book brigades in every stairwell to move physical collections to upper floors. The building had to be shuttered by the end of the day, and there was no estimate of when it might reopen. On the one hand, a key benefit of campus being downstream from the reservoir is that flooding is usually mitigated. On the other hand, when flooding does occur, it can persist for days or weeks. Back in 1993, water poured over the spillway uncontrollably for four weeks.

With top-tier services in good shape, the library IT disaster response team quickly developed plans to restore the second tier (critical to library operations), which included access to networked drives, intranet, and desktop computers. Barring an unimaginable catastrophe, the library's server room was itself not in danger of flooding; if the water reached the building, however, power and networking would be unavailable and the servers would be offline and physically inaccessible. In order for the library to continue to provide services to campus under these circumstances, the server environment would need to be rebuilt in a new location on higher ground.

The team decided that the best available option was to relocate existing production equipment. With several hours remaining before the building closed, there was enough time to power the servers down gracefully and move equipment to the College of Engineering. The racks could not be transported while fully populated because of the weight of hard drives and backup power supplies. Under close supervision of the library's lead system administrator, a team of volunteers—mostly programmers from central IT—helped tear down the servers and carefully transport drives, battery supplies, and half-empty racks to the engineering building. At the same time, another team of volunteers—mostly academic technology staff from central IT—helped move 150 desktop computers and monitors to a storage area. As luck would have it, a new fleet of library computers had just arrived and were still in their original boxes, which made them easy to transport. Fortunately, librarians for the most part had adopted best practices and kept essential work-related files on network storage, so individual desktop hard drives were not a priority.

To the outside world, library servers appeared to be offline for just a few hours, from the time network engineers removed building switches after underground utility tunnels were breached until the VPN that routed the library's subnet to the engineering building was activated. Top-tier services (critical to university operations) were fully online by the end of Friday, and second-tier services (critical to library operations) were available by the end of Saturday.

Temporary Relocation

The university canceled classes and closed campus to all but essential personnel for a full week.[7] The official campus list of essential personnel was born out of pandemic flu planning and appropriately focused on personal safety and medical communications. The university soon recognized that designating which personnel were considered to be essential personnel varied depending on the situation at hand. Library IT staff worked throughout the week to get temporary systems in place so that nearly all library operations could resume when campus reopened. By Friday, June 20, several more servers were back online. Temporary offices were set up: administration, finance, and human resources relocated to the business library; circulation and reserve to the engineering library; interlibrary loan and technical services to the health sciences library; and media services to the physics library. A farm of desktop computers was set up to allow digital library and IT staff to telecommute over Remote Desktop Protocol; public services staff from the art, music, and main libraries worked either from home or at a bank of business library workstations repurposed for shared staff use.

Classes resumed on Monday, June 23, but the main library and two dozen other buildings remained closed. The main library was certified for occupancy on Monday, July 7, and reopened to the public on Wednesday, July 9. Overall, the evacuation went smoothly, and the library continued to serve campus from a variety of remote locations for a month. The only equipment failure was a USB dongle that had accidentally been left attached to the server and was damaged as the server and rack were carted through a doorway.

Resuming Normal Operations

The recovery process was slow. Although the main library reopened to the public in a matter of weeks, repairs continued for months. The art library remained in its temporary location for nearly four years, finally returning home in 2012. The music library continues to be housed in temporary quarters until a new music building is finished, which is anticipated for the fall of 2016, fully eight years after the flood.

A story like this would ideally end with everything returned to its proper home and resuming normal operations. Just as flood recovery began in earnest, however, the global financial crisis hit, further disrupting campus activities, putting flood recovery funds at risk, and prompting many discussions about "the new normal." In November 2008, then-incoming White House Chief of Staff Rahm Emanuel said, "You never want a serious crisis to go to waste."[8] Inspired by this sentiment, library IT staff looked for opportunities to challenge deeply held beliefs and think strategically. Staff occasionally joked about looking for ways to "turn floodwater into lemonade."

MITIGATING RISK

Though significant resources had been spent prior to 2008 to construct a new server room and upgrade equipment, the flood was a visual reminder that a small departmental server room is not an institutional priority. The sandbag wall that protected the library was impressive. But the sandbag wall on the other side of the library—the one protecting the campus data center—was built to a much higher elevation. During the flood, the library's servers were relocated to the College of Engineering's data center, a superb environment with a fully redundant electrical system, yet even there they needed to be shut down briefly when the chilled-water system failed. The message was clear: To maximize the chance of staying online, or coming back online after a catastrophe, library systems could not remain isolated.

Furthermore, the severe budget constraints caused by the combined effects of flood damage and economic recession had a disproportionate effect on library IT staffing. Even without a formal hiring freeze, the university's commitment to avoid layoffs meant that departments with staff turnover suffered the hardest until positions and funding lines could be reallocated strategically.

The need to embrace and become an early adopter of cloud computing, though neither well understood nor well defined, seemed inevitable. Hosted environments and cloud-based infrastructure were not even mentioned in the 2008 edition of the *Horizon Report*,[9] yet cloud computing was given a one year or less time-to-adoption in the 2009 edition which stated

> Advances in computer science to ensure redundancy and protection from natural disasters have led to data being shared across many different hosting facilities. Improved infrastructure has made the cloud robust and reliable; as usage grows, the cloud is fundamentally changing our notions of computing and communication.[10]

Several library IT services, such as interlibrary loan, have been migrated to vendor-hosted platforms—albeit with the usual mixed reviews. Library systems remaining onsite have now been permanently relocated to server farms in more centrally managed data centers.

One of the most significant post-flood infrastructural improvements was a new state-of-the-art, enterprise-wide data center that opened in 2012. Due to service-level limitations, some library systems remain under the care of the College of Engineering, but the rest have been moved to the new data center. In 2013, the library's server room was powered down once and for all.

These cloud-based solutions created new dependencies that triggered significant revisions to the library IT disaster response plan. The library no longer owns any server hardware. Relinquishing local control has its own disadvantages and requires new and different strategies for disaster response.

LESSONS LEARNED IN 2008

LESSON 1

Plans May Be Worthless, but Planning Is Indispensable

The disaster response plan was helpful to define priorities and set expectations. The lack of specificity in the plan did not prove to be problematic; in fact, it kept the document relevant in an unanticipated situation. Former United States President Dwight D. Eisenhower once stated:

> I tell this story to illustrate the truth of the statement I heard long ago in the Army: Plans are worthless, but planning is everything. There is a very great distinction because when you are planning for an emergency you must start with this one thing: the very definition of "emergency" is that it is unexpected, therefore it is not going to happen the way you are planning. So, the first thing you do is to take all the plans off the top shelf and throw them out the window and start once more. But if you haven't been planning you can't start to work intelligently at least. That is the reason it is so important to plan, to keep yourselves steeped in the character of the problem that you may one day be called upon to solve—or to help to solve.[11]

Because it did not attempt to identify every service or to parse subtle distinctions between what was necessary and what was desirable, the written plan retained a focus on broad concepts, and trusted that the implementation team would work out the specifics based on the situation at hand. Too much detail makes a plan less flexible in unanticipated circumstances.

LESSON 2

In Any Given Disaster, Probabilities Don't Matter

A Galton board (sometimes referred to as a "bean machine") nicely illustrates the central limit theorem where any large number of trials will trend toward a normal distribution curve.[12] But the tool also illustrates that it is not possible to predict the outcome for any single trial. There is a temptation to spend time planning the most likely scenarios. A given disaster, however, is just one random experiment. As the disaster unfolds (or as the ball drops down the Galton board), it is easy to account for all possible next moves. In a real-life crisis situation, however, there is neither time to plan for every outcome, nor is there any benefit in guessing outcomes based on a false premise of the typical situation. No disaster is typical.

LESSON 3
Name a Non-Essential Team Member for Communications

The disaster response plan appropriately described how official communications were to be delivered and received, and named the official spokespeople. During a crisis situation, however, it is also necessary to identify personnel who can serve in dispatch roles. These individuals do not need subject expertise or authority. In fact, IT skills can be a disadvantage because of the temptation to pull these individuals away from dispatch. The lack of non-essential team members was especially noticeable when trying to coordinate with external units that were also busy dealing with the disaster. The library needed a place to stow 150 desktop computers and monitors. A potential location was identified; however, key personnel at that location could not be reached and there was no reliable way to leave a message. A non-IT person who could be dispatched to establish contact and close the deal would have been invaluable.

LESSON 4
Identify a Volunteer Coordinator

When drafting the disaster response plan, no one had considered how to handle volunteer offers for help. Yet, during the evacuation volunteers kept pouring in. A few volunteers were IT professionals who were tapped to help with moving servers; but other volunteers without special IT skills had to be redirected to other efforts such as sandbagging or book brigade. Dealing with these individuals took time away from attending to IT needs.[13] Coordinating the many unexpected volunteers was, at times, overwhelming.

LESSON 5
Essential Is a Relative Concept

The notion of identifying essential personnel was first introduced in pandemic flu planning and carried over to other critical incidents. Upper-level administrators and health and safety experts were deemed essential, but IT support staff were not. This proved to be a problem and was quickly corrected. Even among IT staff, the notion of who was essential changed as the crisis unfolded. At times, desktop support staff or web editors suddenly became essential.

Similarly, despite the best effort to list all essential services, circumstances on the ground can quickly change what is considered essential. When the disaster response plan was drafted, interlibrary loan was considered very important, yet it was not made a top priority. With no access to the physical collections, however, the relative importance of interlibrary loan suddenly increased.

LESSON 6
Prepare for Personnel Changes on the Disaster Response Team

Core team members were selected based on skills and availability, but the catastrophe introduced unexpected variables. No one had anticipated, for example, that it would become important to consider which team members lived on which side of the river, a factor that came into play once closing the last remaining bridge in Iowa City became a threat. Several library staff members commuted to Cedar Rapids, normally a 25-mile drive. But road closures increased the detour to 250 miles.

LESSON 7
Look for Easy Opportunities to Repurpose Resources

Staff located in most campus buildings were instructed to pack up their desktop computers. The library, however, had just received new computers, which had yet to be deployed. Because this equipment did not need to be packed, non-IT staff were able to participate in other disaster response activities (such as relocating special collections materials). In a debriefing after the event, staff noted that another option would have been to repurpose student checkout laptops and issue them to library staff as they left. The disaster response plan should explicitly grant authority to one or more members of the team to make last-minute administrative decisions that might contradict standing policy.

OBSERVATIONS FROM 2013

The Iowa River rises every spring, but in 2013 the water level once again triggered the flood response plan. No IT action was required, but the weather outlook was grim and it was not unreasonable to ponder another building evacuation.

The prospect of relocating library staff and library IT operations a second time seemed overwhelming. But how could that be? Although it would seem that riding out a repeat catastrophe should be straightforward, considering all the lessons learned in 2008, the updated disaster response plan, and the move to a centralized data center—but this was not the case.

OBSERVATION 1
Preparedness and Readiness Are Different

FEMA provides families with a wealth of information about planning and preparing for disasters and emergencies on its web site (www.ready.gov). Families with a communication plan, an emergency kit, and a well-constructed home may be equally well prepared for a tornado or a hurricane, but the specific steps for weathering each storm are quite different. Those in the path of a hurricane typically have a few days to get ready, whereas a tornado forms quickly and causes damage only while it touches ground. Hurricane warnings are issued thirty-six hours in advance; tornado warnings sometimes come after the fact.

With the benefit of hindsight, the library's preparedness was equally strong in 2008 and 2013. The digital library was never at risk. Had there been a sudden flood in 2008, the damage would have been unimaginable, but it still would have been completely reversible. The reservoir upstream, however, made Iowa City's flood experience more like that of a hurricane.

A 36-hour warning still leaves 36 hours of work to do. Better preparedness might mean top priorities are in good shape, but there always will be plenty of second, third, and lower priorities that need reinforcement.

OBSERVATION 2
Planned Obsolescence Changes the Calculus

A disaster response plan for library IT may seem immature when compared to a plan for physical collections. The foundation upon which each plan is built, however, is characteristically different. A campus architect imagines a structure that can easily stand for 100 years or more and will engineer the building's infrastructure accordingly. By contrast, a systems administrator will engineer a digital infrastructure with the assumption that a five-year lifespan is optimistic. Irrespective of the actual or perceived value of the contents contained in a physical versus digital library, the fact remains that the physical library is built on a foundation intended to last for generations and the digital library is built on a foundation intended to be obsolete in a few years. If catastrophic natural disasters are relatively infrequent, odds are high that any physical library infrastructure will need to withstand a handful of disasters over its lifetime, whereas any given digital library infrastructure is unlikely to face even one in its lifetime.

Even though a digital library infrastructure is designed not to last more than a few years, careful disaster planning is still paramount due to the risk and cost of failure. On the other hand, the nature of planned obsolescence inherently changes what parts of the plan are most important. Detailing vendor contact lists and documenting IT dependencies for each business function is not time well spent. The IT experts in charge of recovery would distrust and ignore any list of IT contacts prepared months or years prior to a disaster. Plans for emergency communication, however, will always be crucial because even in the best of times, communication between IT and non-IT personnel can be challenging. When water is surrounding the library or the National Guard is directing traffic away from it, it is self-evident that the collection cannot be accessed, but information regarding IT unavailability can be hard to come by when the technology that enables communication is unavailable.

OBSERVATION 3

No Digital Asset Is Original

With physical artifacts, deciding what to rescue first can be complicated because the value of an artifact varies based on who is doing the valuation. The concept of an item having a fair-market value is predicated on an assumption that an acceptable alternative can be proffered. A replacement might be indistinguishable from an original, but in a literal sense it may be materially different.

Libraries tend to rely on these familiar labels when they talk of "unique digital collections" and safeguarding "preservation masters," which loses sight of the subtlety that digital files are literally immaterial; the first time a file is saved to disk it is already a copy. In day-to-day operations, this distinction is meaningless. The strategy for mitigating against loss of information on disk is multiple copies and frequent backups. No one grieves the loss of a file when another copy is successfully recovered from tape.

While bracing for an impending disaster, however, the lack of originality in a digital file is more salient. In 2008, hundreds of volunteers descended upon the library to save the collection. For months afterward they told story after story about book brigades, the size of the collection, and the arcane dissertations they passed from hand to hand. Hundreds of people were needed to save the print collection, and hundreds eagerly volunteered. Yet no one talked about the digital library.

The major takeaway from both the 2008 flood and the 2013 near-miss is the extent to which a library IT disaster response plan is not a particularly valuable technical resource. Certainly, a plan needs sufficient detail to make sense to an IT professional unfamiliar with the environment. But IT professionals solve IT problems for a living, so trying to solve imaginary problems ahead of time should not be a priority. Rather, the most indispensable sections of the plan document the default solutions to non-technical issues—organizational structure, lines of authority, and—most importantly—human relations.

NOTES

1. Stephen Pradarelli, *Iowa Now,* May 28, 2013, http://now.uiowa.edu/2013/05/ui-taking-steps-guard-against-flooding.

2. *Flood 2008 Report,* Board of Regents, State of Iowa, www.uiowa.edu/floodrecovery/recovery-reports/BOR-080708.pdf.

3. *Flood Recovery—Updated Cost Estimates, 2009,* Board of Regents, State of Iowa.

4. Unpublished report, February, 2012.

5. *The University of Iowa Technology Disaster Plan,* Version 3.1 (November 22, 2004), 9, http://itsecurity.uiowa.edu/bestprac/documents/Enterprise-IT-Disaster-Plan.pdf.

6. Paul Soderdahl, personal communication, June 12, 2008.

7. "Most Faculty Members Told Not to Report to Work Due to Flooding," *Faculty and Staff News,* University of Iowa, June 14, 2008, www.uiowa.edu/~fyi/issues/issues2008_v45/06162008/feature2.html.

8. *The Wall Street Journal,* November 21, 2008.

9. *2008 Horizon Report* (New Media Consortium/Educause), 2008, www.nmc.org/sites/default/files/pubs/1316816013/2008-Horizon-Report.pdf.

10. *2009 Horizon Report* (New Media Consortium/Educause), 2009, www.nmc.org/sites/default/files/pubs/1316814843/2009-Horizon-Report.pdf.

11. *Public Papers of the Presidents of the United States: Dwight D. Eisenhower; Containing the Public Messages, Speeches and Statements of the President, 1953-[1960/61],* (Washington, DC: US Government Printing Office, 1958), 818.

12. Barile, Margherita, and Eric W. Weisstein, "Galton Board," MathWorld—A Wolfram Web Resource, www.mathworld.wolfram.com/GaltonBoard.html.

13. There was a humorous miscommunication when a call for volunteers to handle fragile hard drives was relayed as a request to deal with sensitive data.

Chapter Seven

Digital Disaster Recovery and Resources in the Wake of Superstorm Sandy
A Case Study

Thomas F. R. Clareson

In late October 2012, as we watched televised coverage of Superstorm Sandy inundating the streets of New York and the shores of New Jersey, many in the cultural heritage community who lived outside of the disaster area wondered, "What is happening to their collections?" Those involved in working with technology, data, and electronic resources imagined power outages, equipment short-circuiting, and loss of online collections.

When the waters receded, we learned that the analog and artifactual collections in some sectors of the cultural and creative communities, particularly among artists and art galleries, were devastated by the incursion of water from Sandy. But in the library community, through disaster planning and preparedness coupled with collaboration and recovery, many organizations were able to keep their digital collections safe, or had them back online soon after Sandy's waters receded.

How were the digital collections spared, and where did professionals get their information on digital collection protection in the wake of the storm? And, how did those organizations that were affected by Sandy recover?

THE RESOURCES

A number of local, state, and national information clearinghouses assisted the library and cultural heritage communities before and immediately after Sandy.

The Metropolitan New York Library Council (METRO), which serves New York's five boroughs and Westchester County, has served as an information "hub" for digitization and other emerging technologies for many years. Hurricane Sandy struck on the day METRO was planning to hold its Annual Member Meeting (which it eventually postponed). Although they were not able to communicate with its membership face-to-face, METRO used email, listservs, and social media to get disaster recovery information to its constituents and put stricken institutions in touch with needed resources.[1]

The New York State Library (NYSL) and New York State Archives, part of the New York State Education Department, had dealt with major flooding before. When Hurricane Irene cut a swath through upstate New York and parts of the Northeast in August 2011, Director of Archival Services Maria Holden and Barbara Lilley, Library Development Specialist and Conservation/Preservation Program Officer in NYSL's Division of Library Development, coordinated delivery of information resources before the storm. Once the storm subsided, they acted as matchmakers between damaged facilities and information and assistance resources. Pressed into service again during Sandy, Holden and Lilley helped staff the State Emergency Operations Center, New York State's command headquarters for emergency management, assisting cultural heritage institutions that held electronic and physical collections soaked by Sandy.[2]

In New Jersey, library and cultural heritage institutions in three of the southern-most counties (Cape May, Cumberland, and Atlantic) had also been struck by Irene in 2011. During the time between Irene and Sandy, however, a group of librarians and museum professionals from this region had received intensive disaster preparedness and recovery training through LYRASIS (www.lyrasis.org), the largest library and cultural heritage network in the United States. This workshop series, which included two webinars and four days of in-person training, was sponsored by the New Jersey State Library.[3] At the sessions, participants learned about disaster planning and recovery methods, focusing in particular on the Incident Command System (ICS), a protocol used by emergency managers and first responders at all levels of government.[4] Just over a year after Irene and less than six months after completing their training, these institutions had to deal with yet another disaster.

On a national level, two organizations came to the aid of the cultural community with information, "matchmaking" of resources and damaged institutions, and leads on funding for recovery.

The American Institute for Conservation of Historic and Artistic Works (AIC) (www.conservation-us.org), the national association for conservators, has since 2007 trained and deployed a cadre of cultural heritage disaster recovery personnel through its Collections Emergency Response Team (AIC-CERT) group. These preservation professionals staff telephone hotlines, respond to email pleas with useful information, and, when necessary, deploy onsite to work with damaged collections. Those staffing the emergency hotline in the wake of Sandy spoke of receiving hundreds of telephone calls from artists, art galleries, and cultural heritage institutions in need of information and aid.[5]

Heritage Preservation (www.heritagepreservation.org), the national advocacy group for preserving cultural heritage collections, has since 1995 been convening the Heritage Emergency National Task Force following presidentially declared disasters. This partnership of forty-two federal agencies and national service organizations helps coordinate information and resources for cultural heritage organizations, provides situational awareness reports to federal agencies, and issues guidance to the public in recovering personal collections damaged in disasters.[6]

One of the key initiatives of Heritage Preservation and the Task Force is the Alliance for Response program. In twenty-three cities and states across the United States, Alliance networks are partnerships between the emergency management and cultural heritage communities, providing local information, training, and a structure for recovery assistance when emergencies happen.[7]

In the wake of Sandy, Alliance for Response New York City relied on the partnerships it had established to reach out to the cultural and creative communities. Members of the group conducted damage assessments of flooded institutions and worked with AIC-CERT to establish a Cultural Recovery Center to provide a space where artists and institutions could work on collections recovery. As a follow-up to its work after Sandy, Alliance for Response NYC received funding from the New York Community Trust to launch a two-year effort to develop tools and resources for better communication during disasters and provide further training for a cultural heritage based response team.[8]

These initiatives and resources helped provide a safety net for organizations recovering from Sandy. But how did some of the institutions struck by the storm prepare for and deal with data disasters?

THREE RESPONSE SCENARIOS

In New Jersey, residential areas and public libraries near the coastline were especially hard hit. But a number of organizations survived the storm with little building or data damage.

Cumberland County Library System

The Cumberland County Library system (www.cclnj.org), based in Bridgeton, New Jersey, prepared staff by distributing county emergency telephone numbers, providing staff numbers and methods to get in contact with each other, and implementing procedures that guaranteed data could be restored if servers were damaged.

Technical staff at the main library had experienced severe weather before. They took steps to shut down servers and actually unplugged them to keep surges from damaging the hardware. This is a good option if staff has time and access before a disaster hits. Damage to disk drives from surges could cause corruption and loss of data; although complete and incremental backups provide a certain level of recovery from such loss, being proactive is the best option. This type of damage is not always immediately noticeable, and discovering that hardware is failing weeks later might mean that recent backups would not be reliable for restoring your databases. These issues happen often enough without inviting them. Use of redundant array of independent disks (RAID) technology can also help prevent loss and downtime from a data disaster.

Additionally, the layout for the server room in the main library could be considered a model for other libraries and organizations developing or renovating server areas. The servers were installed on the middle floor of the building (not the lowest level), in a windowless area with interior walls formed by surrounding spaces that had no direct doors from the server room to the outside. The servers are rack-mounted in a cabinet several feet off the floor. There is also a large-capacity Uninterruptible Power Supply (UPS) to allow time to shut down properly when circumstances allow, instead of risking a sudden shutdown from a power loss.

Off-site backup of data is recommended for both digital preservation and digital disaster planning and recovery. The Cumberland County Library system utilized this practice; when Sandy struck, there was a full set of backup tapes onsite in a locked, fireproof box on a shelf well above floor level, which also contained a complete set of backup tapes secured off-site as well as system support and contact information at the time Sandy struck. In case of evacuation of the building during a disaster, procedures to retrieve the fireproof box and cut off battery power to the servers' UPS if there is fire or water in the server area go into effect. The shutoff device is not immediately in the area housing the servers and UPS, which allows the power to be cut if the area is too dangerous to enter due to water, fire, or physical damage. This keeps electricity from the batteries from remaining active, and thus dangerous to firefighters and other first responders.

Possibly the most important step that the system had taken prior to Sandy, though, was to develop a computer and automation disaster recovery plan. The plan lists preventive maintenance and proactive disaster recovery procedures for all hardware, operating system, and application software, as well as resources for telecommunications, network, and desktop support. The system manager is extremely proactive in informing all library staff members about these procedures. In addition, information on support contracts for all library systems is regularly updated.[9]

As part of a library consortium, Cumberland was able to provide a certain level of service to its patrons through other libraries until it could again provide direct service. These facilities also provided some staff workspace during the recovery. Electronic resources such as downloadable audio and ebooks, and remote access to online databases, offer libraries an opportunity to provide some level of service while recovering from disasters. However, these activities may require some cooperation with other libraries, IT departments, or vendors if remote authentication is interrupted.

Eyebeam Art + Technology Center

The recovery of the Eyebeam Art + Technology Center's (www.eyebeam.org) multimedia collection after Superstorm Sandy is documented in a report by Kara Van Malssen of AudioVisual Preservation Solutions.[10]

Eyebeam, located on West 21st Street near the Hudson River, is the leading media art and technology center in the United States. Prior to Sandy's landfall, preparedness steps were taken, including raising equipment off the floor on the ground level and covering workstations with plastic. However, a "toxic mixture of saltwater, sewage, and other contaminants submerged . . . over $250,000 worth of equipment—computers, lighting, printers, and servers," which were "completely destroyed." The report also noted that "15 years of videotape and computer disks containing artworks, documentation of events, and even server backups—essentially Eyebeam's entire legacy," were damaged.[11]

The first people to arrive on the scene moved media away from water and the construction crews who were tearing down walls in an effort to restore the area. Next, recovery supplies were obtained and cleaning plans specific to various types

93

of media were developed, focusing on optical discs, computer discs, data tape cassettes, and videotape cassettes. Spaces were designated for recovery of each type of media, and workflow procedures were tested and documented. Volunteers were alerted by various social media outlets to make their way to the center. Roles were established: overall coordinator, operations coordinator, transport crew, documentation crew, cleaning crew, content experts, media conservation experts, and quality assurance and control personnel. Dissociation between media and label info (separation and confusion between the tapes and their containers) was a problem for which the teams had to be very vigilant throughout the recovery process.

Within three days of the disaster, more than 1,300 media items were cleaned and stabilized by a group of forty people.[12]

Some of the lessons learned by those involved in the Eyebeam recovery included the importance of having item-level inventories and keeping at least one copy of the inventory in printed form. Also, having enough knowledge about the collection to deaccession duplicate items was seen as important. Prioritizing materials to be treated was also a key in the recovery workflow.

Perhaps the most important comment made in Van Malssen's report was this:

> Long-term preservation of audiovisual, multimedia, and digital content requires more than just good storage. . . . To truly be preserved, the content must remain accessible. This means that content needs to be findable in a digital environment, understandable to those who might use it, accessible in a common format, and readable using contemporary technologies. An archive is not simply the collection and storage of data, it is a system of people, policies, and technologies managing content over time to ensure it remains accessible through ever-changing landscapes.[13]

Frederick L. Ehrman Medical Library at New York University

On October 29, 2012, Superstorm Sandy struck the Frederick L. Ehrman Medical Library at New York University's Langone Medical Center (www.nyu.edu/academics/libraries/frederick-l-ehrmanmedicallibrary.html) flooding the basement and lower level of the facility.

The greater part of the library's physical collection had already been moved to off-site storage because of a pressing need for space, and was thus not affected by

Sandy. The onsite collection was either destroyed or was salvaged, refrigerated, and is now in another off-site storage location.

To protect its digital collections, NYU had begun shutting down its servers two days before the storm made landfall, and systems were managed remotely by IT staff working off-site. When the storm hit, however, email and phone systems went down, generators were disabled, and even security card key-readers malfunctioned.

When a few staff members arrived the day after the storm passed, they began to unplug and move computers and servers as quickly as possible. This was well timed, because water contaminated with trash and oil flooded back into the facility on October 31.

Although the Medical Library did not have a comprehensive written disaster plan for its digital collections, it had collaborated with Medical Center IT staff to develop "elaborate plans for the handling of outages." And, before the storm hit, planning was already in process to relocate important library servers to a remote, safe, and secure data center in New Jersey.[14]

The damage caused by Sandy was exponentially worse than a minor power outage, however. In some cases, according to Library Associate Director for Access Resources and Systems Stuart Spore, "no humans could get near some of the servers and digital collections for several months," although some had been removed from the facility and taken to secure/remote locations. Additionally, sixty-five to seventy computers and printers damaged by the storm were moved off-site. But a year later, there was still no place to return them.

Because of the quick action of the staff, a workable level of library services was up and available to users on November 11, 2012, about ten days of the storm. However, at the time the author spoke with Spore, he felt it might be 18 to 24 months from the time Sandy hit until the physical library can re-open. Spore noted that during the year after the hurricane, there had been a great deal of discussion on "what the library should be in the future." Spore said that, as a result of Hurricane Sandy, NYU's Frederick L. Ehrman Medical Library had become "a total digital library overnight," and that transformation had convinced him that a library can go completely digital either as a result of a disaster, or through a planned transition.

"I think the greatest lesson of Sandy is that, given a sufficiently harsh environmental disaster, a digital library can recover much faster than a physical library can," said Spore. "It's pretty easy to knock a digital library offline, but with normal attention it's back online quickly. If you knock a physical library out, it can take months, or years, to recover, if it recovers at all."

"There's a range of vulnerabilities in digital library environments, so how they're managed matters," Spore continued. Before Sandy, the library was "very vulnerable [to disasters] and our path to recovery had to be improvised. And yet, we were back in more or less full operation eleven days later."

Spore urged library and IT staff to pay special attention to three factors:

- "Have the systems you need as secure and safe as you can make them;
- Cultivate an intelligent, dedicated, and creative systems staff; and
- Stay positive and be ready to communicate and motivate under dire and stressful circumstances."

CONCLUSION

Across the three cases noted here, communication, pre-planning, "planning on the fly" immediately after an event, outreach to volunteers and experts, and knowledge of valuable information and resources were important factors in the organizations maintaining or re-implementing their services. These five factors can help anyone charged with stewardship of digital collection when disaster strikes.

NOTES

1. Jason Kucsma, METRO, discussion with author, June 29, 2013.
2. Maria Holden, New York State Archives, discussion with author, May 14, 2013.
3. "Regional Emergency Response Network," https://www.lyrasis.org/ LYRASIS%20Digital/Pages/Preservation%20Services/RERN.aspx.
4. Incident Command System, www.fema.gov/incident-command-system.
5. American Institute for Conservation of Historic and Artistic Works, Disaster Response and Recovery, www.conservation-us.org/publications-resources/ disaster-response-recovery/aic-cert#.UnKsuRBGb18.
6. Heritage Emergency National Task Force, www.heritagepreservation.org/ programs/taskfer.htm.
7. Heritage Preservation, Alliance for Response, www.heritagepreservation.org/ afr/index.html.

8. New York Alliance for Response, http://heritagepreservation.org/afr/NewYorkCity/index.html.

9. Susan D'Ottavio, CCLS, conversations with and e-mails to author, April 23, and August 12, 2013.

10. Kara Van Malssen, *Recovering the Collection, Establishing the Archive,* (New York: AudioVisual Preservation Solutions, 2013), 1, www.avpreserve.com/wp-content/uploads/2013/05/RecoveringTheEyebeamCollection.pdf.

11. Ibid., 5.

12. Ibid., 21.

13. Ibid., 22.

14. Stuart Spore, NYU, interview with and e-mails to author, August 28, August 29, and October 28, 2013. All comments attributed to Spore are drawn from this conversation and correspondence.

RESOURCES

American Institute for Conservation of Historic and Artistic Works Collections Emergency Response Team (AIC-CERT). www.conservation-us.org/publications-resources/disaster-response-recovery/aic-cert#.U-uA1WP2-oY.

Federal Emergency Management Agency. *Collection: Rebuilding after Katrina and Rita.* www.fema.gov/media-library/multimedia/collections/173.

Heritage Preservation. www.heritagepreservation.org.

LYRASIS. https://www.lyrasis.org.

Van Malssen, Kara. *Recovering the Collection, Establishing the Archive.* New York: AudioVisual Preservation Strategies, 2013. www.avpreserve.com/wp-content/uploads/2013/05/RecoveringTheEyebeamCollection.pdf.

Disaster Communication Planning Template

This template can be used as a basic disaster communication plan when responding to the notification of a disaster.

Action	Date/Time	Assigned to	Time Completed	Notes
Following onset of incident, disaster response (DR) team leader will decide when to activate the internal communication plan and alert the DR team.				
DR team leader launches DR team and briefs the team about the situation.				
DR team meets to assess situation, develop approach and strategies.				
DR team includes the Head of Information Systems in discussions—this department may have special needs and inputs.				
DR team leader provides administration with an overview of the scope of the disaster and information about immediate needs for restoring services.				

Action	Date/Time	Assigned to	Time Completed	Notes
DR team leader identifies and briefs designated spokesperson. Discuss response and messages.				
Spokesperson prepares initial internal and external communications.				
Messages and strategy reviewed and approved by administration.				
DR team and spokesperson deliver initial internal and external messages.				
DR team leader informs library staff as soon as possible. Provides information about where and when to report to work.				
Social media team updates library website and social media with information on the emergency.				
Spokesperson coordinates meetings with media and delivers approved messages to vendors, suppliers, the media, staff families, and the community.				
Library Director communicates with insurance companies, consultants, contractors, disaster response companies, and other outside assistance.				

Action	Date/Time	Assigned to	Time Completed	Notes
DR team obtains regular status reports from other teams involved in the response and recovery.				
DR team prepares and distributes status reports regularly on the situation.				
DR team prepares and delivers regular updates to stakeholders, government agencies, and other relevant entities.				
Spokesperson prepares and delivers messages on resolution of the emergency.				
DR team and spokesperson provide ongoing updates to internal and external parties as the situation is resolved.				
DR team is advised by senior management that the emergency is over.				
DR team prepares and issues post-disaster reports as needed to internal and external parties.				
DR team conducts post-disaster review of and revision to the disaster communication plan.				

Example—University of Notre Dame

In 2009, during the first week of fall classes, the University of Notre Dame experienced an extended, widespread communication outage that affected the entire campus. A fire in a utility tunnel destroyed a substantial portion of the campus communications infrastructure. Notre Dame's response to and handling of the incident is an excellent example of the benefits of a well-designed disaster response plan, the creation of a formal incident response and emergency operations center that incorporates an ongoing disaster response and business continuity initiative, and repeated testing of the various plans using realistic emergency simulations.

For more information on this incident, see Dewitt Latimer, "At Least It Wasn't a Football Weekend: The Notre Dame Tunnel Fire," *EDUCAUSE Research Bulletin* 2009 (20), October 6, 2009.

Example of a Basic Disaster Communication Plan for a Public Library

Staff: If Library closes due to major service disruption, Library Director will notify the Library Disaster Team. Director will use Staff phone chain and email blasts if available.

Public: Library Director posts status through Police and FEMA phone alert, digital sign, and community broadcast alerts.

Schools: Library Director contacts School Superintendent.

Voicemail Update: Library phone message has to be changed onsite using login codes.

Library Website: Tech Coordinator will update the Library website and the staff intranet site for alerts.

Social Networking: Communication Coordinator will post on Library's Facebook page and Twitter account and contact press.

Library Communications: Library Director contacts the State Library, the state library association, and local library consortia.

Media Communications: Library Director is authorized to speak with the media, with Library Board President as backup.

Contributors

LIZ BISHOFF is president of the Bishoff Group, LLC. Previously she was the director of Digital and Preservation Services of BCR; special assistant to the dean of libraries and head of the Office of Sponsored Programs, University of Colorado, Boulder; vice president for Digital Collection Services at OCLC; and former executive director of the Colorado Digitization Program. Bishoff has worked with libraries and museums in several states, including Alabama, Kansas, South and North Carolina, Missouri, Minnesota, New Mexico, New York, and Tennessee, on various aspects of their collaborative digitization initiatives. She led the development of collaborative best practices in metadata, including the Western States Metadata Dublin Core Best Practices. Bishoff is a faculty member for NEDCC's School for Scanning, Persistence of Memory and Stewardship of Digital Assets.

MARSHALL BREEDING is an independent consultant, speaker, and author. He is the creator and editor of the Library Technology Guides website (www.librarytechnology.org) and the lib-web-catsonline directory of online libraries (www.lib-web.org). His monthly column Systems Librarian appears in *Computers in Libraries*; he is the editor of ALA's *Smart Libraries Newsletter,* and has authored *Library Journal's* annual "Automation Marketplace" feature since 2002. He has authored nine issues of ALA's *Library Technology Reports*, and has written many other articles and book chapters. Breeding has edited or authored seven books, including *Cloud Computing for Libraries,* published in 2012 by Neal-Schuman, now part of ALA TechSource. He regularly teaches workshops and gives presentations at library conferences on a wide range of topics.

THOMAS F. R. CLARESON is a senior consultant at LYRASIS. Clareson joined PALINET (which became LYRASIS in 2009 when PALINET and SOLINET merged to form a new organization) in October 2005. He led PALINET's digital collections creation and management services, preservation services, and consulting activities, and was responsible for establishing new services and funding sources, grant writing, and outreach to the museum and historical society communities. In his current role at LYRASIS, Clareson consults nationally and internationally on preservation, digitization, special collections/archives, remote storage, funding, and advocacy issues.

DONIA CONN is the workshop program and reference coordinator at the Northeast Document Conservation Center (NEDCC) and one of the creators of dPlan. She presents preservation, disaster planning, and recovery workshops throughout the Northeast. She also speaks to local institutions about preserving family collections. Conn answers calls on NEDCC's 24-Hour Disaster Hotline to help institutions in the face of disaster. As reference coordinator, Conn answers technical inquiries relating to preservation topics from around the world. She earned her MLIS with an Advanced Certificate in Conservation from the University of Texas-Austin and has interned at Trinity College, Dublin, and at the Folger Shakespeare Library in Washington, DC. She worked as a rare book and paper conservator in academic institutions across the United States before joining NEDCC.

DENISE O'SHEA is head of access services and systems at the Harry A. Sprague Library of Montclair State University in New Jersey. She recently presented on Disaster Response and Recovery Planning at Back in Circulation Again, a biannual national conference for circulation managers and staff hosted by the School of Library and Information Studies at the University of Wisconsin, Madison. Her library background includes working in public, special, and health/science libraries. She earned her master's degree in library science at Rutgers University and is currently pursuing a second master's degree in public and organizational relations at Montclair State University.

PAUL A. SODERDAHL is associate university librarian for information technology at The University of Iowa. Soderdahl holds a BA in mathematics and a BM in music from Northwestern University, and an MS in technology-based music instruction from the University of Illinois at Urbana-Champaign. His MA in library and information science is from The University of Iowa. Soderdahl has been active in the Library and Information Technology Association, and has authored several articles on technology in academic libraries. He has served in a number of capacities in various Ex Libris users groups, including as a steering committee member of the SFX/MetaLib Users Group and the Ex Libris Users of North America.

Index